THE
TOUGH
STUFF

The
Tough
Stuff

Seven Hard Truths
About Being a Head Coach

Cody Royle

Library of Congress Cataloging-in-Publication Data

Names: Royle, Cody, author.
Title: The tough stuff: seven hard truths about being a coach / Cody Royle.
Description: Toronto: 9479180 Canada Inc., 2021.
ISBN: 9781660114443

Printed in the USA

Book design by Fredrick Haugen

To Mum,
Thank you for your love and generosity.
You prepared me to face The Tough Stuff.

To Poppy Royle,
My favorite thing is to sit and listen to your stories.
You've always taught me to think differently about the world.
I hope this book makes you proud.

Why I Wrote This

In April 2019, I was invited to Las Vegas to present at the Leaders In Sport conference. The content team at Leaders asked me to speak about talent optimization, but gave me the freedom to explore that broad topic without too many boundaries. I imagine they expected me to return with a presentation on how to build an environment that allows your players to achieve peak performance. Instead, I spoke about optimizing coaches.

Nestled in between Toronto Blue Jays psychologist Dehra Harris, the Air Force's equivalent to Jester from Top Gun, and poker legend Daniel Negreanu, I was certainly the least recognizable face on stage that day. I have no doubt I was the least popular presenter as well. For 45 minutes, I stood on stage at the UFC Performance Center and told the world's top coaches that they were short-changing their athletes by not taking better care of themselves.

"For too long, the 'do as I say, not as I do' methodology has prevailed," I told them, "where self-care rules are rigidly imposed on players while the coaches eat at the McDonald's drive-thru and slink into the hotel bar for four pints before bed."

While the seed was planted that day, my speech was never intended to become a book. The coach optimization idea lay dormant for over a year until the COVID-19 lockdown engulfed the globe and shut down professional sports. For the first time ever, every head coach in every elite sport in the world had ample time. Better yet, we were all going through exactly the same thing at exactly the same moment. There was an immediate commonality and a thirst for connection and idea sharing. The more coaches I reached out to, the more called me back seeking a conversation about what they were going through.

With time to reflect, the overwhelming theme from the coaches that I spoke to was a realization that they'd been winging it for most of their careers. Each season blended into the last, their personal lives were frazzled, and the competitive demands of the game had created the perfect excuse for failing to take care of themselves: There's never enough time.

This book is my declaration that there is enough time, and the 'do as I say, not as I do' era of coaching is over. We must opt-in to this new world of leadership and come together with our players as allies in performance, not adversaries. After all, our ability to perform as coaches is a substantial factor in their ability to perform as players.

In the coming pages, I'll unpack how coaches can become high-performers. To get there, though, we must deal with some confronting realities—a few hard truths. The toughest pill to swallow may be that the problem is us. We must look in the mirror and begin to make the necessary changes for ourselves. No one coming to our rescue.

Who am I?

Looking back now, it appears that I was a born coach. I grew up in Canberra—Australia's capital city—and rugby league was my first obsession. When I was six or seven, I'd open a notebook and write out two teams on opposite pages (sometimes even drawing the team logos), then take my book out into the front garden of our house and play the game. Up and down the garden I'd go, playing the game on behalf of both teams. There'd be substitutions, injuries, and tactical adjustments—anything my young mind could conjure.

When my family moved to Melbourne, my imaginary games in the garden continued, only now the sport was Aussie Rules. At high school I won a state championship in 4 x 100m relay, and earned state selection in Aussie Rules at U15, U16, and U18 levels. But for all my foot speed on the track and ball skills on the field, it wasn't quite enough for me to go professional in the AFL. By my early twenties I'd fallen out of love with playing the game, but not with writing out teams in my notebook.

I began coaching with the Calder Cannons in the elite junior system, and had a new goal in mind: become the first AFL coach who never played professionally. That became difficult to achieve when I moved to Canada, but working with elite athletes in Aussie Rules was still possible through AFL Canada's performance teams. Since 2012, I've been working to transform our men's national program from being an afterthought for our players into being a life goal for them and their families.

On top of my own head coaching experience, I've spent the better part of the last decade interviewing dozens of the world's most thoughtful coaches to learn from them and incorporate the ideas that are most relevant to me.

One of my first ever blogs was a Q&A with Gary Kirsten, India's Cricket World Cup-winning head coach. My blog site ultimately led me to writing my first book, *Where Others Won't*, which included, among others, input from Buffalo Sabres head coach Ralph Krueger, and former Phoenix Suns head coach Igor Kokoškov. The success of the book spawned a podcast of the same name, which allowed me to extend my leadership learning by interviewing bestselling authors like Adam Grant and Daniel Pink; business executives like Patty McCord and Chip Wilson; as well as sporting legends like Anson Dorrance, Joe Dumars, and Michael Gervais.

On top of these formal conversations there have been countless lunches, dinners, Zoom chats, and beers that have sharpened my perspective and challenged my firmly-held beliefs about being a head coach. I've met rowing coaches, curling coaches, triathlon coaches, squash coaches, and lacrosse coaches. I've been invited to share what I've learned at national conferences and with world champion teams.

Six-year-old me would be beside himself if he knew the phone numbers of many of his heroes would end up in his address book, and that he'd get to spend so much time, as an adult, writing down teams in his notepad.

Why should you listen to me?

I believe I'm the perfect person to write this book for three reasons. First of all is that I'm a head coach, too. Working at the elite amateur level, I have the ability and the leeway to test advanced coaching ideas away from the kerfuffle of the media and the money. On a small scale, I deal with all of the problems written about in this book. You will feel it in my writing that I've grappled with the subjects we're about to explore. From hard-won experience, I've tried to sharpen my own coaching practice. That is the foundation of my suggestions. This book isn't written by an academic looking to prove his thesis; it's written by a coach with his battle scars still visible.

The second reason you should listen to me is that I bombed out of the system. I never made it. I'm not quite an outsider, but not a close insider. I'm a close outsider. For the last decade, I've been the person watching from a bird's eye view, taking in context that those in the industry either can't see, or don't want to see. No one actively working in the professional ranks would ever write this book. It's too gritty and vulnerable, and unless you're a championship-winning coach with job security, the industry is still too cut-throat to promote disruptive ideas like the ones you're about to encounter.

Thirdly, this book isn't populated by me. It's written by you. The topics I've chosen are your ideas regurgitated back to you. These are the things that head coaches call me about, email me about, and ask for my advice on. I've collated the ideas and sought out additional color and context for the stories, but this is the stuff you've been telling me you're struggling with.

This is *The Tough Stuff* because it gets to the core of who we are as human beings, and it's difficult to dig around down there. More than anything, I hope you'll read this book with an open mind, and I'm excited to hear your stories of how you've been prompted to start thinking differently about your own coaching performance.

*"Studying leadership is way easier than leading.
I completely underestimated the pull on my emotional
bandwidth, the determination to stay calm under
pressure, and the weight of continuous problem-solving
and decision-making... and the sleepless nights."*

Brené Brown

The Seven
Hard Truths

1. Everyone thinks you're an idiot

Head coaching isn't what you expect. When you're the one in the spotlight, every word will be scrutinized, every decision will be dissected, and every accomplishment will be questioned. There is nowhere to hide, and often some of your harshest critics work alongside you.

2. Your fiercest rival is yourself

Despite what you might think, your toughest battles aren't with worthy opponents on the field of play. Your ability to navigate the emotional toll of being a head coach will define your legacy more than wins and losses.

3. You don't possess the God Particle

Overbearing control only leads to obsession, neuroticism, and distrust in your organization. To master head coaching, you must learn the art of letting go.

4. You're not a coach

Having your identity wrapped up in coaching is damaging and unsustainable. The foundational piece of your career journey isn't figuring out who you are as a coach, it's figuring out who you are as a person.

5. You're hired for your brain

As experts in human development, coaches are well aware of how to optimize the brain for elite performance. We pass those lessons on to our players and forget to adopt the learnings for ourselves. Becoming a high-performance knowledge worker requires that we rethink how we spend our time.

6. Every word counts

Communication is not merely explaining a training drill or delivering a rousing half-time speech. It's infinitely more complex. Every inflection, text message, silence, and behavior communicates something to someone, whether you want it to or not.

7. Tactics don't really matter

Teams don't win because of their tactics, they win because of their cohesion. Building better teams requires coaches to rethink preparation and focus on connection rather than correction.

*"If you don't have the courage to walk alone,
others will not have the courage to walk with you."*

Apoorve Dubey

Everyone thinks you're an idiot

Being the boss

"It's not all football like it was when you were an assistant coach. The problem some people don't understand is that when you're the head coach, you're the face of the organization," mused former Carolina Panthers, Denver Broncos, and Chicago Bears head coach John Fox.

In an interview published in *The Athletic*, Fox described in detail how even some of the most seasoned assistants are left unprepared for the full rigors of the head coaching position. "You're not going to be locked in a dark room watching video and coming up with plays," Fox added bluntly.

Everything changes when you're the one in the spotlight. You can go from a sought-after coaching candidate one day, to facing cynicism and scorn the very next day. Many new head coaches are caught out by not being able to retreat into their office and diagram their way out of a challenge.

It's one of the oddities of elite sport that an entire career path can render someone surprised about the challenges they'll face when they're in the top job. In this chapter, I'll outline the vast array of outside pressures that arise when you're the boss.

Unpreparedness

As a player, Tony Granato was one of the NHL's best wingers, scoring 264 goals across fourteen seasons with the New York Rangers, Los Angeles Kings, and San Jose Sharks. He is perhaps best remembered for forming one of the league's most deadly line combinations with Wayne Gretzky and Luc Robitaille in Los Angeles.

After retiring and spending a season away from the game, Granato missed the camaraderie of an NHL locker room and decided to join Bob Hartley's staff as an assistant coach with the Colorado Avalanche. In 2002, the Avalanche had won eight consecutive division titles. They were hellbent on keeping the streak alive, which would allow the team an opportunity to replicate their Stanley Cup victory two years earlier.

By December, though, the Avs had slipped thirteen points behind their division rivals Vancouver, and the organization decided to remove Hartley as head coach. "As they fired Bob Hartley in one room, they pulled me into another room and said, 'Hey, we're firing Bob, and we want you to take over,'" Granato told me on an episode of *Where Others Won't*.

Three months in, Granato felt he was barely settling into the demands of being an assistant coach; figuring out how to run training drills, organize meetings, and get videos cut up for the players. All of a sudden, he was the boss.

"It was a big surprise, but I understood why the change was made," Granato said. He added reflectively, "Our team should have been performing at an elite level, but was just mediocre." The team Granato adopted featured Patrick Roy, Joe Sakic, Peter Forsberg, and Rob Blake—all of whom were instant Hockey Hall of Famers. Complementing them was the league's top goalscorer, Milan Hejduk; three-time Team Canada Olympian Adam Foote; and an elite young playmaker named Alex Tanguay.

You'd imagine with such a talented team, the Avalanche would have had a sizable support staff to help manage the transition and smooth the bumps for a young and inexperienced coach like Granato. But you'd be wrong.

"I had Jacques Cloutier, one of the most loyal, hard-working, dedicated assistant coaches, and we didn't have anyone else on staff.

It was him and me running an NHL team for two months before we were able to hire Rick Tocchet to join us as a second assistant coach," Granato told me.

One head coach.

One assistant coach.

Running one of the greatest NHL teams ever to be assembled.

Duties that Granato and Cloutier would've gotten their hands dirty with are nowadays their own departments requiring full-time staff and PhD-level prerequisites.

Being shot out of a cannon is never the ideal start to your head coaching career, but handing Granato the reins worked for Colorado. On the last day of the regular season, the Avalanche overhauled Vancouver, securing their prized division title and another chance at the Stanley Cup.

For Granato, despite his unpreparedness, he remains thankful for the opportunity to shepherd such a splendid team. "Was I experienced enough to handle some of the things that came at me? No way," he admitted, "But do I believe I was the right person for the job at that time? Yes, I do."

There's a lot more to it than you think

Former Liverpool and England captain Steven Gerrard has also spoken about his on-the-job learning, suggesting that his first head coaching job with Glasgow Rangers came before he was ready.

During an interview on *The High Performance Podcast*, Gerrard discussed how he thought he knew a lot about what to expect because he'd watched his coaches closely throughout his playing career. "When you step into being a manager yourself, there's a lot more to it than you actually think," he admitted.

Unlike many who believe their playing career to be a right-of-passage, Gerrard took a different line of thinking, suggesting he was at a disadvantage because he was a player. "Coaches like José Mourinho and Brendan Rodgers, the reason they're so good at what they do—and they're so slick—is because they've had 20 years of coaching experience. I won't have that luxury because I played. For me, it's going to be a different type of journey," Gerrard said with conviction.

Pressed by the podcast hosts on whether there were any specific instances that he found particularly difficult to navigate, Gerrard was quick to the draw: "Addressing the Rangers squad for the first time was one of the most nervous talks I've ever done."

Few know soccer at the elite level better than Steven Gerrard. Yet, despite having captained every team he'd played on and addressed his teammates hundreds of times, he was still caught out by the subtle differences of being the boss.

Fifty problems a day

Steven Gerrard's longtime England teammate, Frank Lampard, is now the head coach of Chelsea. While playing together, the two often struggled to sync up, but they agree on the difficulties of arriving on the head coaching scene.

The BBC quoted Lampard as saying, "I realize now that head coaching is much harder than playing in terms of it being all-consuming. Between twenty-five players in the squad, staff in the building, problems with different departments, a head coach gets fifty problems a day. It's so far removed from just football."

Frank Lampard was a child prodigy in English football, watching his father compete over five hundred times at the top level. He'd spent his entire life observing and playing football at the elite level, yet was another that was caught out by the unique demands of head coaching.

Your impact on others

Dan Quinn hadn't called a timeout at any level of football until the Atlanta Falcons hired him as their head coach. Upon ascending to the top job, he paid particular attention to how people treated him. "When you become a head coach," he told me over the phone, "you think you're the same person, but others view you differently."

Something that many head coaches notice is the immediacy of behavior change from those around them. Subconsciously, power structures have an impact on our physical behavior. For instance, when you have a chance encounter with a celebrity at a coffee shop, your heart begins to beat faster. Or when the CEO walks into the office, you sit up a little straighter and enunciate your words a little clearer. And when the head coach walks into the gym, the players lift their weights a little harder.

The first change Quinn noticed was that the nature of his relationships with his staff changed. "Naturally, there's going to be some separation with your assistant coaches because you're now responsible for their professional livelihoods. That's something you just don't have to deal with when you're an assistant yourself."

The second change Quinn observed was the effect of his time on others. He relayed to me that he found this to be a crucial point. "It might be just another 10 minutes to you, but you have to realize that it might be the most important 10 minutes in that other person's day. It's important to be mindful of those experiences with players and staff, and for you to be present in them," he explained.

The impact you have on those around you—sometimes with your presence, other times with your words—is a learning curve for head coaches. You'll notice that it's a consistent theme throughout this book and is re-visited in the sections to follow.

Everyone's a critic

As Dan Quinn noted, one of the most significant changes head coaches experience is the relationships with their staff. It's often those same staff who can be among the most critical of you, and where you spend a lot of your energy.

Recently, I visited with a professional team to watch them practice and learn from their coaches. As I stood off to the side, observing the session, a strength and conditioning coach came to introduce himself to me. After the introduction, he listed off all the grievances he had with the head coach and told me all the things the coach had done wrong last season. The strength coach was unaware that it was the head coach who'd invited me down.

Former Arsenal high-performance director Darren Burgess tells me that even a legendary coach like Arsène Wenger wasn't immune from internal criticism. Wenger was known for bringing all-new preparation and nutrition standards to the Premier League but still faced disapproval from recent sport science graduates. "We'd have kids just out of school questioning Arsène's training session because the players did slightly more running than originally planned," Burgess told me during our conversation. "I'd have to assure some of our staff that Arsène changed the sport and had won more trophies than we'd had birthdays, so he knew a thing or two about player loading," Burgess added.

The problem, Burgess says, is that criticism snowballs quickly through gossip and whispers. "You get journalists questioning the coach, then the fans start to question the coach, then people inside the club start to question the coach. It conditions everyone to think that way, and all of a sudden, everyone's a critic," he concluded.

Of course, it's not just the staff who work for you affected by your position; it also impacts the people you interact with the most—your players.

Different things (to different positions)

Recently, NFL.com journalist Jim Trotter set out to identify the coaching traits that players found most important. To get a well-rounded picture, he polled one player from each different position group, with each player also playing for a different team. Each was allowed to name three general traits they wanted to see from their head coach.

Here are the answers:

Quarterback: Listening, communication, connectivity
Running back: Honesty, steadiness, flexibility
W*ide receiver:* Player trust, honesty, student and teacher
Tight end: Leadership, honesty, scheme
Offensive lineman: Consistency, organization, loyalty
Defensive lineman: Communication, leadership, competitive
Linebacker: Leader of men, detailed playbook, will to win
Defensive back: Philosophy, knowledge, staff assembly

What shines through is that there is as much consistency as there is inconsistency in what the different playing groups held dear. Head coaches are expected to be consistent but flexible, a student and a teacher, as well as being a ruthless competitor that also connects emotionally. This paints a marvelous picture of the complexity of head coaching, and should provoke thought on how something as simple as a player's position may affect how they think about us.

Being unpopular

When we hired a new head coach for AFL Canada's national women's team, I was lucky enough to sit on the interview panel. More than anything, I was interested in hearing one thing from each of the four candidates: How do you feel about being unpopular?

A coach's role isn't to make everyone happy; it's to make decisions that help the team realize their goals. Often those decisions are unpopular. When talking about successful coaching, we often overlook the fortitude required to stay the course and not get distracted while dealing with the wash-up of tough decisions.

You'll be ridiculed before you're revered

Ange Postecoglou arrived at Japanese soccer club Yokohama F. Marinos having already coached two different Australian club teams to back-to-back national titles, as well as leading the Australian men's national team to continental success in the AFC Asian Cup.

Despite Postecoglou's accomplishments, translator Naoki Imaya estimates that 95% of the players didn't believe in the new coach's methods. Yokohama F. Marinos are one of the larger teams in Japan's top tier of soccer, and after three games of Postecoglou's reign the team had yet to register a win. The pressure was on.

Imaya says that in those early days the players would come to him and question Postecoglou's competence; 'Come on, Naoki, are you sure this guy's got any idea?' the players would ask. "Obviously I had to stand firm," Imaya said in an interview published in the Brisbane Times, adding, "I said to them, 'He's a top coach so listen to him. If you want to talk to him, we'll go and talk to him together.'"

Postecoglou's first year was rocky yet transformational; the club's worst league finish since 2001 was somewhat brightened by a Cup Final appearance. Marinos were scoring lots of goals but were conceding them in droves as well. Yet the building blocks for future success were well-and-truly in place.

In his second season, Postecoglou's coaching methodology was validated in the most convincing way possible—Yokohama's first J1 League championship in fifteen years.

In the words of Liverpool head coach Jurgen Klopp: "It's not so important what people think when you arrive, it's much more important what people think when you leave." I dare say the players at Yokohama F. Marinos will have a positive opinion of Ange Postecoglou when he eventually departs.

You may just be ridiculed

It's not only your staff and players who can be skeptical, either. Australian society is unforgiving of those who stick their necks out and attempt to reach new heights of achievement. For dreamers like Ange Postecoglou, they're often met with chortling laughter and a 'who do you think you are?' mentality. Don't dream too big, they imply.

Another head coach who has experienced this mentality is former Australian netball team head coach Lisa Alexander. After leaving her post as head coach of the Aussie Diamonds, she boldly declared that she wanted her next role to be a head coach in the men's AFL competition.

Different sport. Different gender.

Alexander has never coached a game of Australian football at any level, but after ten years and 102 Test matches in charge of the country's netball team, her rationale was that she knows how to facilitate elite environments. "I could easily improve one of the bottom six teams in the AFL right now if they wanted to take a chance," she told me.

I have no doubt she could. Others aren't so sure.

As you can imagine, Alexander's daring proclamation was met with snickers from the media and general public alike. I captured a small handful of the comments posted to one news article:

- If she wants to coach an AFL team, maybe start by working your way up and getting experience in footy.

- She coached in a completely different sport. I'm going to apply for a job as a dentist with my teaching degree.

- I've got a driver's license, but that doesn't mean I can fly a Boeing 747.

- How many times has she run a kicking drill?

- Using her logic, an AFL coach could easily coach a Premier League side. Both sports kick a ball.

"A lot of people say I need to start at the bottom and work my way up," Alexander explained to me, "But that would be like the CEO of JP Morgan being made to start at the bottom if they joined Facebook. Even though they probably can't code a website, you'd still make them the CEO because they're a great CEO."

Despite the criticism and mockery, Alexander is not at all disheartened. "I chose that goal because it's a stretch for me, and I'm excited by the challenge," she said. "It's a glass ceiling, and I'd like to pave the way for other women to get into high-performance coaching."

Dealing with fame

Connacht Rugby head coach Andy Friend has enjoyed a long and illustrious career in northern and southern hemisphere rugby. Having coached high-profile teams like Harlequins, the Brumbies, Suntory Sungoliath, and the Australian men's Sevens team, Friend has spent the better part of two decades in the public eye.

When I asked how relative fame had impacted him, Friend took the conversation beyond himself and spoke openly about the knock-on effect to his two sons:

> "I remember saying to my kids that they'd read things in the newspaper that would make me look like a miracle worker, or make me look like a dud. I'd remind them that I'm none of those things. I'm just Dad. When they were young I don't know if they understood that I had a job that people had an opinion on, but my wife and I just tried to normalize it as much as possible for them."

Rugby only professionalized in the 1990s, so while big clubs from other sports have transcended their cities and are chasing global opportunities, many rugby clubs still operate as their local area's heartbeat. As Friend explains, this dynamic brings its own unique sort of pressure. After a farewell home game for Brumbies legends Stirling Mortlock and George Smith (which they won 31-3) there was a big send-off on the field. As Friend headed down the race, someone called out to him: 'Hey, Friend, you're a ********!'

"My son Jackson was walking beside me and he looked at me and asked whether I knew the man who'd yelled out. When I told him I'd never seen him before in my life, Jackson said, 'Well then, he's a fool, why would he say that to you if he doesn't even know you?' He was exactly right," Friend reminisced.

Being the target of verbal abuse after an emphatic home win is ridiculous, but there are other landmines that head coaches and their families must navigate.

"Every now and then we'd have some people who would become 'friends' because they wanted to hang around with the kids of the Brumbies coach, or the wife of the Brumbies coach," said Friend, whose status was particularly heightened in that role given he was born-and-raised in Canberra.

"Sometimes, people just want to be associated with the title, not the person. We had a family codename for those people so that we could get rid of the hangers-on from our lives," he added with a wry grin.

The business

If you ask a head coach what they dislike most about their job, they'll often respond with a simple answer: the business.

It's ironic because filming an advertisement, attending a corporate event, doing a broadcast interview, or keynoting a lunch for season ticket holders is the money-generating activity that pays your salary and allows your professionalism. Nonetheless, they are a series of mandatory activities that further distance coaches from doing what they love most—coaching players.

Previously, much of the business was still at arm's length from the team itself, but with the boom of the content industry, new demands further blur the lines between sport and entertainment. The new wave of behind-the-scenes documentaries, for instance, provides both opportunity and annoyance.

"When the club agreed to the deal with Amazon, of course, we were worried about it," said former Tottenham Hotspur head coach Mauricio Pochettino, who was fired during the filming of the *All or Nothing* documentary series. Talking prior to his exit, Pochettino was firm about the added intrusion: "It is tough to have a camera in your office. It is so complicated, it is another thing to worry about."

With the content wars only beginning to warm up, behind-the-scenes sports content isn't going anywhere. Rather than viewing this new media as invasive, perhaps we should be looking to utilize its unique power. After all, many of the subjects featured in the recent documentaries have come out favorably with fans and players. Rather than being a hindrance, perhaps we can start to use these business opportunities to show elite players why they should play for us, and why on-the-fence fans should root for us.

The face of the franchise

Earlier in this chapter, I wrote about some advice longtime NFL head coach John Fox offered to new head coaches. Fox expanded on the specifics of being organization's new spokesperson and the additional responsibility it brings: "The owners are looking for a guy who's the face of the franchise," Fox said, "Someone who's going to interact with the building, whether it's on the personnel side, the administration, or the PR department."

The realities of head coaches being 'the face of the franchise' aren't lost on decision-makers in global sport, with a handful of teams adapting their interview process to include media elements.

Take England men's soccer team head coach Gareth Southgate, who was subject to a three-hour, five-person firing squad during his interview. According to FA chief executive Martin Glenn, Southgate was asked to review his four-game stint as caretaker coach, which led to "some pretty feisty opinions from the more technical people in the room," he said. Explaining the process to the BBC, Glenn noted that the intent was to see whether Southgate's "powers of analysis stand up to scrutiny," adding, "It's really important for the England team and is important for anyone in what is a high-pressure role."

Analyzing games and managing the expectations of key internal stakeholders is one part of the role, but as John Fox notes, being the organization's spokesperson is an entirely different kettle of fish.

Facing media scrutiny over every detail of every game can become taxing, and the only role that I can think of that might command greater media attention than the English soccer team is the head coach of the New York Yankees. In an effort to acknowledge this unique proposition, the Yankees have started utilizing the media as part of their hiring process. During their 2018 coaching search, they released all five candidates' names and subjected them to a conference call with the broadcasters that cover the team.

General Manager Brian Cashman explained to the *New York Times* that the process has multiple benefits. Firstly, the news media may dig up information on a candidate that the Yankees' own background search missed. Secondly, is the ability to observe how the candidates handle questions from the largest press contingent in Major League Baseball—something a Yankee coach is required to do twice a day, 162 times a year (more, if they make the playoffs).

For a team in a pressure-cooker environment like the Yankees, baking the media demands into their job search is an impressive innovation. It immediately eliminates candidates who interview well but cannot handle the other demands that come with coaching one of the world's most-recognized sports franchises. There's more to it than just baseball acumen.

The worst call in history

We often associate media pressure with coaches whose teams are losing, but sometimes you're lampooned even when you're a serial winner. One particularly outrageous example springs to mind, which came at the expense of Seattle Seahawks head coach Pete Carroll, who is one of only three coaches to have won a Super Bowl and a college national championship.

After Super Bowl XLIX, in which Seattle lost to New England, Carroll was pilloried after a controversial late-game play call went wrong. Down 28-24 and at the 1-yard line, Carroll had quarterback Russell Wilson throw the ball rather than hand it to star running back Marshawn Lynch. The consensus was that Lynch would have run the ball in for a touchdown, and Seattle would have won the game, but instead Patriots cornerback Malcolm Butler intercepted Wilson's pass and the Patriots went on to claim victory.

The mainstream media gleefully carried their pitchforks at the front of the angry mob, with Fox Sports calling it "the dumbest call in Super Bowl history," while *USA Today* ran the headline: **What on Earth was Seattle Thinking with Worst Play Call in NFL History?**

The worst play call in NFL history? Really?

Even highbrow media got in on the act, with *The New Yorker* running an article titled "A Coach's Terrible Super Bowl Mistake."

From a coaching perspective, the Seahawks made the right call. The analytics boffins tended to agree, but it wasn't enough to stop the onslaught of abuse. As poker player Annie Duke points out in her book *Thinking In Bets*, Carroll and the Seahawks were victims of what's called 'Resulting', whereby we equate the quality of a decision with the quality of its outcome.

Quite frankly, the worst call in history wasn't the play call, it was the editor's call to run that headline.

Was it a good plan?

Some coaches struggle with the level of misunderstanding from outsiders, particularly given the lack of access to what the team is trying to achieve. At a recent press conference, Manchester City head coach Pep Guardiola responded to a journalist's question by evoking the notion of Resulting:

> *"Sometimes you have a plan, and it works, but you don't win. Sometimes you have a plan, and it's a disaster, but you win. The perception is that it's a good plan if we win, and not so good if we don't, but it depends on our opponent, and on the quality of our players and how they decide to play."*

Despite the truth to his words, Guardiola's perspective was wildly unpopular among many journalists on Twitter. As the self-appointed guardians of everything that is true, journalists have long struggled with being outsiders to the inner sanctum of pro sports. For coaches, media misanalysis becomes a source of frustration because it inevitably sways the opinions of those making decisions in the boardroom, and other key stakeholders around the club.

A common misnomer in pro sports is that it's a results business, but in reality it's a process business. Organizations get into trouble when the process they committed to and agreed upon is hijacked by a nervous executive who flinches at something as meaningless as a media member's game review.

Peer pressure

It's not simply journalistic opinions that head coaches need to deal with, either. Sometimes, your most savage critics are your peers. When he was the head coach of FC Barcelona, one of the world's most popular soccer teams, Pep Guardiola was subjected to unwanted analysis from fellow coaches, a dynamic he has been outspoken about. In an interview, Guardiola aired his distaste of the excessive prying from his coaching brethren:

> *"It's not easy to coach at Barça. I still get so pissed off because even coaches from other teams make comments about what I should be doing. What do they know? They aren't there every day in every training session, dealing with players who lack confidence, players going through divorces, players with problems at home. There's a million things that can affect the performance of a player and the people on the outside know nothing about it."*

Whether it's journalists, executives, or fellow coaches, one thing you know as a head coach is that you can't make everyone happy. We've already agreed that behind-the-scenes sports documentaries aren't going anywhere, so perhaps it's time that we learn to better communicate why we've made certain decisions, and expose people to the context and detailed thought that went into it. Whether they want to listen or understand, of course, is another question.

Pressure from above

Former NFL executive Michael Lombardi once told me something profound: "New coaches need to spend more time understanding why there was a job vacancy in the first place." What he means is that too many coaches jump right into a new job without taking time to truly comprehend the problem they're solving. The last coach was talented as well, so why did they get it wrong? Was it genuinely performance-based, or were there other underlying factors? Was it something as shallow as opinions in the media?

Oftentimes, something is broken beyond just the team's win-loss record: organizational alignment, the environment, the locker room, the ownership. You may find an owner that's self-aware enough to tell you the truth during the interview process, but it's presumptive to think that occurs in all situations.

With that in mind, it's good practice to canvas opinions from all corners of the organization so you can have a more robust picture of the state of play. More than anything, understanding the problem you're solving allows you to create time and energy to tackle more pressing issues that will arise.

The pressure of insta-expertise

Consider the vast amount of topics we ask head coaches to have in-depth knowledge and instant expertise in: sport science, safety, understanding elite athletes, game knowledge, statistics, languages, psychology, communication styles, group dynamics, coaching craft, human behavior, conflict resolution, learning environments, player welfare, recruitment strategies, financial prudence, game operations, media management, and negotiation.

And that's before we get to the social and political climate, where coaches are looked upon to guide young men and women through vast and complicated issues that spring into prominence like Black Lives Matter, aboriginal land rights, or Hong Kong's independence movement. Coaches were even asked to provide their opinions on the deep science of the COVID-19 outbreak.

And we go into the job expecting to be able to 'just coach'.

Advancing the cause

Something that won't come up in coaching education is how to navigate being asked to defend your politics, ethics, and social causes. And rest assured, when you're the boss, you will be asked about them.

For his political views, Manchester City head coach Pep Guardiola has been called a hypocrite. In particular, the media have criticized Guardiola for supporting the democratic independence movement of his native Catalonia while at the same time working for a democracy-quashing monarch in United Arab Emirates crown prince Sheikh Mansour.

In the case of Minnesota Lynx head coach Cheryl Reeve, she realized her own hypocrisy after listening to a mentor. In March 2019, legendary Notre Dame women's basketball coach Muffet McGraw announced that she'd never hire another man to her coaching staff. "People are hiring too many men. Women need the opportunity. They deserve the opportunity," McGraw stated firmly.

For Reeve, McGraw's words cut deep. There is already a gender disparity amongst WNBA head coaches, and in a span of two years, two of Reeve's senior assistant coaches (both men) were lured away to coach their own teams. Reeve had always considered herself an outspoken advocate for female coaches, but through her sustained success was inadvertently creating a pipeline of male head coaches.

"When Muffet took that stance, as much as I advocate for women, it dawned on me I was doing a poor job to the cause of more women in coaching, particularly the WNBA," Reeve told the Minneapolis Post.

Despite what we like to think, sport does not play out in a bubble. We are intertwined in life and society and politics. Being a head coach is a position of power and influence, and despite your best efforts to 'just coach' you'll be called upon to represent something or to speak up for someone.

The pressure to give up on people

University of Alabama football coach Nick Saban is renowned for two things: his winning and his rants. Having won six national championships at two different schools and coached the Miami Dolphins in the NFL, Saban commands respect whenever he speaks about football or life. One of his most famous media sermons came in 2014 when he was asked about giving players second chances.

"When somebody does something wrong, everybody wants to know how you're going to punish the guy. For 19- and 20-year old kids, there's not enough people out there saying to give them another chance. So, I'm going to give a speech about this: Where do you want him to be? If a guy makes a mistake, do you want him to be out on the street, or do you want him to be at school, graduating?

When I coached at Michigan State, I had a player named Muhsin Muhammad. Everybody at the school, every newspaper guy, everyone was killing him because he got into trouble. They said there's no way he should be on our team.

I didn't kick him off the team. I suspended him and made him do punishments. Muhsin graduated from Michigan State, he played 15 years in the NFL for the Carolina Panthers, he's the president of a company, has seven children and his eldest daughter goes to Princeton. So, who was right?"

As Saban concluded his monologue, the silence from the media throng was palpable. Perhaps they were scared. Perhaps they were embarrassed. Perhaps they were reflecting on their roles in cutting down young men who'd made juvenile mistakes.

Ultimately, what Saban was pointing out is that he refused to take part in the condemnation and hard exile that many in elite sports rush to when a player messes up. The pressure to give up on people, young people, can easily become crushing. It takes bravery and gumption to stand on stage in front of a national (sometimes international) audience and stick up for a young man or woman who has made a mistake. But isn't that what leadership is?

Being the boss

Everything changes when you're the one in charge. There are no opportunities to tiptoe into the background to avoid the spotlight. If you let it, the outside pressure can become all-encompassing before you even get to your day job—coaching players.

England Rugby head coach Eddie Jones summed it up best in his autobiography, stating: "Coaching is difficult. You're supposed to know everything and offer constant belief and hope to a huge number of mostly complex individuals. At the same time, everyone thinks they can do the job better than you. You're never short of someone telling you what you're doing wrong."

Key Takeaways

1. You're not an idiot!

2. Head coaching is not what you expect. Most of what you do as an assistant coach doesn't prepare you for the outside pressures placed on a modern head coach.

3. Pressure comes from all angles, and sometimes your closest staff turn out to be your most savage critics.

4. The content revolution is only just beginning. Behind-the-scenes content isn't going away. Learn to love it.

5. There is no place the media won't go; you should prepare to discuss your private life, your politics, and your personal history.

*"Unresolved emotional pain is the
great contagion of our time—of all time."*

Marc Jan Barasch

Your
fiercest rival
is yourself

2

Dealing with The Weight

When speaking about the pressures experienced by head coaches, observers often mistakenly refer to it as the weight of expectation. They focus on the outside scrutiny—the pesky topics we discussed in the last chapter—but neglect to dig much deeper than that.

I'm yet to meet a head coach whose own expectations didn't far exceed those of outsiders. What's debilitating for coaches isn't so much the weight of expectation; it's the weight of caring.

As former Carlton Blues head coach Brendon Bolton points out, "Some of the issue is that AFL coaches have got fifty players that they treat like sons. On top of that, they've got fifteen coaches that they're really invested in. All of a sudden they've taken on a hundred people, let alone their own family and themselves."

'The Weight' is the cumulative stress and anxiety brought upon by caring deeply about people, and the impact and influence your role has on them. I believe this to be true of both emotionally intelligent coaches and those who display more narcissistic patterns (they do care underneath all the snarling and ego).

As we'll explore throughout this chapter, your ability to navigate The Weight probably has a larger impact on your coaching performance than any game plan or recruiting strategy ever will. And, if not approached in the right way, with the right tools and the right support infrastructure, your battles with yourself can start to become incapacitating.

The stuff you don't see

It's a problem that we so rarely get to hear about the emotional toll of head coaching. When we do, it's buried in the pages of a post-career autobiography. Even then, memoirs are reserved for serial winners, and publishing companies know that the formula for selling more copies is to tell glorified stories about on-field success, not dark portrayals of emotional hardship. These surface-level depictions of head coaching overlook critical pieces of the puzzle and rob future generations of meaningful learning opportunities.

A quick look at the Amazon charts shows this phenomenon in action: roughly 80% of the Top 100 sports coaching books are about tactics. I believe we dramatically overestimate the importance of X's and O's and shockingly underestimate how crucial it is to equip coaches with the right tools to navigate the emotional toll. After all, coaches spend their days worrying about the wellbeing and performance of every single person in the organization, knowing in turn that their wellbeing has barely even crossed anyone's mind.

It also cannot be lost on us that the democratization of information has created a dynamic where emotional intelligence, not tactical intelligence, is the fierce new battleground. This shift is societal as much as it is sporting, but is the root of many of the struggles modern coaches encounter. Namely, we have a mismatch; a generation of people taught to suppress their emotions and adhere to authority is leading a generation of people taught to express their emotions and speak up to authority.

That mismatch is not going well.

How can we expect head coaches to develop emotional intelligence and self-awareness in others when they aren't even equipped to recognize or navigate their own emotions?

With no emotional security, no job security, and no executive suite accountability, head coaches are thrown into the fire and expected to work wonders. We're hired based on our process but measured on our wins and losses. A veritable merry-go-round has been created, but no sane person in any industry should want the term 'merry-go-round' attached to their leadership hiring.

The hot seat

Not long after I interviewed them for this book, both Ben Olsen and Dan Quinn were on the hot seat. They were fired within three days of each other.

Despite being well-respected and much-loved, it was fascinating to observe in real-time the vitriol directed their way as their teams underperformed. There was a frightening disassociation that Ben and Dan were real people, and a chilling belief that—because they're compensated handsomely—attacking them personally was justified.

Movements have begun to shield players from receiving this type of abuse, but it must not be forgotten that coaches are also subjected to unacceptable levels of degrading and dehumanizing abuse (and not just when they're losing, sometimes when they're winning, too).

A life-saving intervention

Shortly after Ben Olsen and Dan Quinn were fired, I watched on as North Melbourne Kangaroos head coach Rhyce Shaw requested extended leave to deal with personal issues. Ultimately, he stepped down a week or so later.

Shaw is from one of the AFL's famous families, and had a long and successful career as a player. A popular and well-respected figure around the league, he'd just completed his first full season in charge of the Kangaroos. Recognizing that he wasn't doing well mentally, Shaw reached out for help and was able to get the treatment he needed to keep himself fit and alive. It so easily could have ended differently.

Whether it's the vitriol faced by Ben Olsen and Dan Quinn, Rhyce Shaw's near catastrophe, or any one of countless other warning signs, it's become abundantly clear that the support infrastructure around head coaches in elite sport is woefully inadequate.

The silence

I don't believe it's hyperbole to say we're dancing with death right now, and my question is why we are waiting for a head coach to end up in the ground before we do something about it. How is it acceptable for a head coach to be forced from the game, and we just sweep it under the rug and continue on like nothing happened?

Remaining silent on The Weight does a disservice to the entire coaching community, and we're at a point where lives are on the line. To move forward, I believe it's time for us as coaches to break our social conditioning and begin to talk about the emotional toll we deal with. To show that it's possible, I'll go first.

The unexpected call

I can still feel the blood rush from my head and the tingling feeling that ensued. I was standing in the middle of an open-plan office, phone to my ear, when Jeremy was finally able to get the words out, "Ned passed away last night."

I'd just returned from a two-week vacation in Melbourne. My uncle had drunk himself to death a few months earlier and I wanted to spend some time at home to be with my grandfather and my mother, both of whom I idolize. Despite missing my wife, it was one of the best trips I'd ever been on. I spent time with my best friends, visited with three AFL clubs, and went to a Fatboy Slim concert.

Two days after I got back to Toronto, I got the call from Jeremy. Ned died by suicide.

His name was Brian Correia, but we called him "Ned" because he had a big bushy beard like Ned Kelly, the famous Australian outlaw. Our Ned was one of the most natural Canadian-born AFL players I'd seen in my decade of coaching here. He assimilated to our cultural environment as seamlessly as he glided across the ground when he ran, and despite being new to our setup he was already a central social figure.

The night he passed, he set his personal best at the squat rack. He left behind three young daughters. His loss affected so many that at his funeral about one hundred people had to stand in the lobby of the church because both the pews and walkways were full.

The day of the call, myself, Jeremy, and our team manager, Brad, spent that evening calling as many of our forty-five players as we could reach to tell them the news first-hand. It was a haunting experience that I wouldn't wish on anybody, but it tells you about the quality of character of Jeremy where—as a fellow player and one of Ned's best friends—he volunteered for the task of making the calls.

What quickly became apparent to me was that I wasn't doing alright. The Weight got to me. Earlier, I defined The Weight as the cumulative stress and anxiety brought upon by caring deeply about people, and having a starting midfielder and one of your cultural heartbeats pass away three months before a major tournament is about as traumatic as it gets. I felt unprepared and too immature to lead a group of young men through the grieving process.

Thankfully, I was able to put some people around me who would understand the dynamic of being a young leader in a team sport. I'll be forever indebted to Cameron Schwab, Meg Popovic, and Mark Popovic, who dropped everything to take my calls and offer both solace and advice.

I'm choosing to tell this story because it's difficult. I much prefer to honor Ned's memory by using his story to help others, including leaders who may find themselves with the same burden I did. Unfortunately, it's a burden that's becoming all too common.

I'll carry the weight of Ned's loss with me for the rest of my life. I still cry intermittently and get sad when I see his Facebook profile. There is one small tactic, though, that helps bring a smile to my face. To honor him, we gave Ned a suffix. Whenever one of our team says his name, it must be accompanied with "...what a f**king legend."

That feeling of fraudulence

Australian actor Hugh Jackman is synonymous with the role of Wolverine and is an Academy Award away from completing the famed EGOT (Emmy, Grammy, Oscar, Tony). Despite being one of the world's great performers, he recently described his feeling of unease at being invited to appear on his favorite podcast, *The Tim Ferriss Show*. Jackman says his inner voice was saying to him, "You've done alright in your career, but you're not someone who people are going to listen to on Tim Ferriss."

If you've never heard of imposter syndrome, it's the belief that you're unworthy despite evidence of high achievement. It's a feeling of phoniness and a fear of being exposed as a fraud. I had imposter syndrome after Ned's passing, and having spent the last ten years interviewing high-achievers across a multitude of disciplines, one of my biggest takeaways is how rampant it is.

Hugh Jackman went on to vividly explain his feeling of inadequacy in greater detail: "I think the nervousness comes from a habitual thought pattern, which is thinking that I'm not that good. I say this to be completely open and honest about the fact that I have doubts about being good enough." Then, in true imposter syndrome fashion, he apologized for "taking the conversation off-piste."

Yes, Wolverine gets imposter syndrome.

And here's the thing: coaches get it, too.

Just like other high-achievers, some head coaches doubt themselves and remain unsure why their skills and decision making have rendered them successful. In private conversations, many can recall a botched team speech early in their career where having the whole team staring at them made them self-conscious and a blabbering mess.

The word 'fraud' comes up a lot when coaches don't deliver wins on the board, but many coaches don't have to wait for outsiders to make them feel like they're not worthy—the 'I'm a fraud' conversation has already taken place in their head.

Miami Heat head coach Eric Spoelstra has spoken openly about his battles with imposter syndrome. As the hand-picked successor to ten-time NBA champion and Hall-of-Famer Pat Riley, expectations were always going to be high for Spoelstra. "My first two or three years as a head coach, I really battled and struggled with feeling like I wasn't ready and didn't belong," he told ESPN.

Just as he was beginning to feel settled, Miami signed LeBron James and Chris Bosh.

For Spoelstra, even four successive trips to the NBA Finals, including back-to-back championships, wasn't enough to truly rid him of the feeling of fraudulence. In fact, it took LeBron James leaving the team for him to finally identify and connect with his purpose as a head coach.

"I had a big six-week reflection on my purpose in this profession," Spoelstra said, divulging that it was during this period that he realized his purpose was to help his players achieve their dreams, and help the organization develop a culture that they believe in. "That was the biggest transformation for me. After that, I didn't give a thought to the impostor syndrome," he added.

What we must understand about imposter syndrome is that it doesn't just impact newcomers or those early in their careers. It impacts the established, the elite, the decorated, and it can rear its head at any time. If Hugh Jackman and Eric Spoelstra can get it, so can you.

"We feel guilty if we don't work enough"

To cure imposter syndrome, many coaches work themselves to the bone. The mentality becomes: 'I can prove that I deserve to be here by working my butt off!'

In early 2019, Leeds United head coach Marcelo Bielsa sent a scout to spy on the training session of rivals Derby County. Asked to explain his actions, the notoriously meticulous Bielsa said that he did not have bad intentions or wish to cheat, and that he always sent people to observe his opponents. "We feel guilty if we don't work enough. Watching [the opponent's training] allows us to have less anxiety," Bielsa admitted through a translator.

Here's my translation of the translation: 'We did our work so well that we had too much time leftover and felt bad. Rather than being proud of our great work and sending our staff home to their families, we decided to re-validate what we already knew using covert CIA tactics in order to win a football game'.

As head coaches, we must hold ourselves to a higher standard than to allow this kind of paranoia. It makes me wonder whether the professionalism of coaching has been good for our discipline, or whether it's simply created more time for us to obsess over the wrong things.

The curse of busy

In 2013, Baltimore Ravens head coach John Harbaugh agreed to let ESPN follow him around and document his game-week schedule minute-by-minute. The article followed health scares for then-fellow head coaches Gary Kubiak and John Fox, and aimed to show the rigors NFL head coaches put themselves through in-season.

The NFL is unique in its short seasons—6 months from pre-season games to Super Bowl. But it's wrong to assume that head coaches use their time off to rest and recharge.

On the week he was tracked Harbaugh had time allocated between roughly 5 AM and 11 PM each day, and slept on the couch in his office on Sunday, Monday, and Tuesday nights to reduce the time spent commuting.

Harbaugh spoke to his wife every day, albeit for 10 to 15 minutes at a time (and anywhere between 5:30 AM to 9:55 PM), and protected time for Bible study, calling his brother, and watching game film with his father. To his credit, he was diligent about exercise, although he spent one 45-minute treadmill session reviewing offensive game plan diagrams.

However, what stood out most to me about the article wasn't the time allocation, it was Harbaugh's personal riffs on how he thinks about his preparation and performance.

On sleep: "There's always more you could do, but if you don't sleep, you can't function."

On talking to his wife: "It is the best time of my day—a chance to step away from everything and remember what's important."

On working out: "I exercise as much as I can. It's a time when I can relieve some stress and think. In this job, you sometimes feel invincible, and that's just not reality."

On time with his daughter: "My time with Alison on Fridays is kind of like my sanctuary. Just for a little while, it's a chance to get away from everything."

Harbaugh's riffs point to a man who loves what he does and attacks his career with passion, but is screaming out for a chance at greater balance. Unfortunately, the lack of any similar articles since 2013 points to how coach wellbeing continues to be something we're willing to overlook in the name of entertainment.

The Slog

In 2017, Los Angeles Clippers head coach Doc Rivers was noticeably unwell. For months, he pushed through weakness, tiredness, and vomiting. Rivers was having IVs just to get through games, but they were unable to re-energize him enough to allow him to stand for the full 48 minutes.

Rivers missed a game completely in January and was still unwell by late February, sending assistant coach Mike Woodson to do the postgame press conference after an overtime win against the Charlotte Hornets.

In a Los Angeles Times article titled "NBA's Scary Secret: Job Stress is Destroying the Health of Some of The Best Coaches," Rivers reflected on the tumultuous period, noting: "I almost thought about quitting because I had no energy. It definitely affected my day-to-day ability to coach—and to live. This job is tiring. And then you're sick on top of it. I didn't do any favors for myself."

Since his episode (which turned out to be a parasite), Rivers has paid more attention to his wellbeing, returning to pregame meditation and scrapping postgame alcohol. He's also become a watchful eye for other coaches in the league, calling at least one rival who he'd observed as looking 'frayed'.

This phenomenon is what coaches often refer to as 'The Slog'. It is the cloudiness of cross-timezone travel, different hotels every week, and takeaway food. It is the haze of mentally preparing for Dallas and New Orleans while reviewing your games against Los Angeles and Phoenix all while being on a flight from Boston to New York. It is a world where you don't know what day it is, you just know it's 'game minus one' and that you haven't spoken to your mother in god-knows-how-long.

Where's home?

The first thing you accept as a head coach in elite sports is that it's a job without security. Through success or failure, you know you're going to have to uproot and move to a new suburb, city, or country.

"But it's not just you," Andy Friend reminded me, "It's your wife, your kids, your family. You need a very patient and understanding partner, which, in my wife Kerry, I most certainly have."

The Friends have recently settled into their nineteenth different home across a 25-year coaching career, this one in Galway, Ireland.

More than just demanding that his family follow him around the world, Friend actively includes his wife and kids in the decision making when assessing a new coaching job. He says they have a checklist of three questions:

1. Is the job right for our family?
2. Does the job allow me to grow as a coach?
3. Will the job financially reward us for what we're about to put ourselves through?

The checklist is progressive, he adds, noting that "if number one is a no, we don't even consider number two, and if number two is a no, we don't even consider number three."

Friend has held head coaching roles in England, Ireland, Japan, and Australia, and confesses that he's always tried to instill a family ethos that wherever they are, that's home.

"When the global pandemic hit, people asked me and my wife if we were going to go home, but our home is Galway. We have a house in Canberra, but our home is wherever we live. When you look at it through that lens, you're never away from home," he concluded.

The bubble

There was no better depiction of how much coach wellbeing is an afterthought than during the NBA bubble in Orlando, Florida. To protect against the spread of COVID-19, the NBA resumed their regular season in the sanctity of Disney World, with the 22 teams still in contention all moving in for the duration of their seasons.

At the beginning of the second round of the playoffs, players could choose whether to bring their loved ones into the bubble. Referees were allowed one guest from the Conference Finals onwards.

The coaches?

They weren't so lucky.

Coaching staffs from the Los Angeles Lakers and Miami Heat, who played against each other in the NBA Finals, went 96 days without any personal contact with family or friends.

Denver Nuggets head coach Michael Malone was scathing of the NBA, calling it "criminal in nature" for the league to leave the coaches in such a situation. On Day 60 of the bubble, prior to his team's playoff game against the Los Angeles Clippers, Malone went off-script at a press conference, railing: "I think I speak for me, I speak for my coaches, and probably all the coaches down here. This is crazy. I miss my family."

"I hope my kids can get their dad back"

The EFL Championship Playoff Final is often dubbed 'The World's Richest Game', with the winner guaranteed Premier League riches the following season.

After winning the Playoff Final, Fulham head coach Scott Parker gave an interview that was quite telling in its honesty. Asked whether he could enjoy big moments like this, Parker responded: "You can't really. You get to Saturday night and, by the time you're drinking a beer and having a little bit of Chinese food, you're all of a sudden thinking about what the next game is. We are in a profession where you win a game, then you lose the next one and you're deemed a failure. You realize that you have to always be at the top of it and always planning."

Scott Parker is tipped for big things, but winning The World's Richest Game may very well be the crowning glory of his coaching career. His one wish? "I just hope that after tomorrow I can sit down with my family. I hope I can sit down with my wife and kids, who for last year have probably been on eggshells, and get their husband back and get their dad back, and I can get to do the things that I want to do," he said with a somber tone.

You could sense relief in Parker's voice, but it was not joyful relief, it carried a sense of pain. His morose tone was sad, and not indicative of what you'd want to hear from a young man who'd just coached his team into the most lucrative competition in the world.

There, but not there

Doc Rivers has been in the NBA since 1983. He played for fourteen seasons, becoming an All-Star and representing Team USA along the way. He's coached for twenty-one seasons, capturing Coach of the Year in his first season with the Orlando Magic, and winning an NBA championship with the Boston Celtics. Recently, Rivers stepped down as head coach of the Los Angeles Clippers after seven seasons in charge, but within days he was hired as the new head coach of the Philadelphia 76ers.

His NBA life is one of dizzying highs, new cities, and extreme sacrifice.

"To be good at this job, you have to make some pretty tough life sacrifices," he said on Netflix's docu-series *The Playbook*. "I have five kids and I missed a lot of their stuff because I was working. Sometimes I missed their stuff and I was there. I was at the event, but my head was thinking about 21 Down Twist [a play] and I'd be scheming for the next game."

Part of Rivers' challenge has been his unparalleled success; in thirty-five seasons as a player and coach he's only missed the playoffs a handful of times. The demands of an NBA regular season are taxing enough, but those extra months of playoff basketball add up over decades.

Coaching will be all-encompassing at times, but we must ask ourselves whether it needs to be that way all the time? Is your team going to run 21 Down Twist better because you're thinking about it during your daughter's ballet recital, or will your team improve more by you being present in your daughter's life?

"Are you getting the sack tomorrow, Dad?"

While Andy Friend's coaching career is an undoubted success, he's seen his share of failure, too.

He's experienced what it's like to get fired. Twice.

"I got sacked on a Tuesday. We played a Monday night game and when I got home the CEO called to ask me to resign," he recalled. After a heated discussion where he refused to stand down, Friend walked down the hallway. "My youngest son, who was 13 at the time, called out to me: 'Are you okay, Dad?' He'd heard the call, and when I asked him if he was okay with it, he said 'I'm okay if you're okay'. I told him it would be big news at school tomorrow, but that I'm okay with it."

Friend says the process of being fired shone a spotlight on how quickly life moves on when you're not there. "One day you feel like you're an integral part of the team. You have this sense of worth and importance. You feel that if you're not there, the team can't function," he said buoyantly. "Then you get fired and you watch the news the next day, and the team still functioned."

One indelible truth of coaching is that the leader is finite and the club is infinite. It can all go away very quickly if you get swept up in your own self-importance and lose sight of the bigger picture.

"The bottom line is you're a support person there to make the players better. If you're not there, they'll lean on another support person," Friend added with finality.

Some much-needed perspective

After coaching Montréal Impact in their inaugural season, Jesse Marsch took six months off to backpack around the world with his family. Circumnavigating the world, they visited 32 countries— staying in hostels, guest houses, and on friends' couches.

Marsch talked about the experience on Gary Curneen's excellent podcast, *Modern Soccer Coach*. "To witness how different cultures live on a daily basis, see random acts of kindness, and how people looked out for us, it was incredibly rewarding," Marsch recounted.

While the travels enriched Marsch's life and brought his family closer together, it also gave him perspective on his career as a head coach. "At the time, I felt the weight of the world from my first coaching experience with Montréal, but when I was in India or Nepal or Laos or Jordan, nobody cared what was going on in Major League Soccer. Nobody knew my name, or cared if I won or lost, or what my record was. Nobody cared!" he said emphatically.

Marsch says it's probably not what the fans want to hear, but 'Nobody cared' was an important lesson that has shaped his mindset ever since. With some much-needed perspective, Marsch realized that there is a limit to the importance of what it is you do, a limit which is difficult to see clearly when you're in the daily hustle.

Micro-traumas

On one of our regular Zoom calls, German women's rowing head coach Tom Morris said something to me that has been ruminating with me ever since. He offered, "As humans, we experience micro traumas on a regular basis, which means we must also experience some version of micro-PTSD."

Naturally, when we think about traumatic stress we get swept up in major life-altering events, but we should not be so casual in overlooking the effects of more everyday occurrences. If we've learned anything from the discussion around concussion in sport, it should be that small, repetitive blows can add up to something much more significant and debilitating over time.

It rips your heart out

Team selection is often forgotten as a contributor to the immense burden head coaches carry with them. Asked what he considers the hardest part of being a head coach, Manchester City head coach Pep Guardiola knew his answer instantly. "The worst thing, by far, is when you cannot let your players play. There are many players who deserve to play, but we can only play eleven. That's the toughest part of our profession," he said, shaking his head in sorrow as he spoke.

As a player, I used to hammer my coaches if I was left on the bench or dropped from the team. I wish I'd known how complex and arduous team selection was for them. I've had to learn the hard way through my own coaching experience.

When you care about your players, taking away their opportunity to play rips your heart out. You know that whatever your rationale, it's not going to be good enough to offer them solace. The toll this takes on coaches is something you cannot fully comprehend until you've been in the chair and made those tough decisions for yourself.

You feel you've let so many people down

Former Atlanta Falcons head coach Dan Quinn has experienced how The Weight can impact you even when you're successful. He told me that it was crushing to lose the Super Bowl because it felt like he'd let so many people down—players, coaches, the owner, and fans.

In Super Bowl LI, Quinn's Falcons came within 57 seconds of winning, before being overrun by the New England Patriots. "That's a heavy weight to carry with you, and it stays with you until you get to be back in a similar situation and show that you've learned from it," he opined.

The team never got a chance to prove what they'd learned. They went back to the playoffs the following year, but were eliminated by the eventual Super Bowl champions, the Philadelphia Eagles.

The loneliest man in Australia

The prologue of Eddie Jones' autobiography is a sprawling chapter that culminates in him coaching Japan to a monumental upset win over South Africa at the 2015 Rugby World Cup. It wasn't the win that piqued my interest, though, it was a passage on the third page that probably slipped through the cracks for most readers. For effect, I've bundled together two closely related quotes from that passage:

> "I prefer not to talk to anyone on the [team] bus. It's a lonely job and I'm used to its solitary nature. When I became Australia's head coach in 2001, Rod Macqueen, my predecessor, explained the challenges of the job. His final words hit home. 'You're now the loneliest man in Australia'."

Eddie Jones is one of the most revered and respected coaches in his sport, and is one of few rugby coaches that is recognizable to the outside world. Writing his life story, which includes Rugby World Cup finals with three different nations, and too many trophies to count, and it took him just three pages to begin to talk about the loneliness of his work.

It's a bizarre reality to consider that head coaches feel a crushing level of loneliness despite spending a majority of their time around other people. It's perhaps even more bizarre when you consider they're the most recognizable faces in any organization.

However, when it comes to loneliness—particularly for high achievers—it appears we've been trying to solve the problem in the wrong way. In researching her book, *The Happiness Track*, Stanford science director Emma Seppälä found that almost 50% of people identified themselves as either 'often' or 'always exhausted' due to work. Stunningly, the research also found a significant correlation between work exhaustion and loneliness. In an article for *Harvard Business Review*, Seppälä explains: "This loneliness is not a result of social isolation, as you might think, but rather is due to the emotional exhaustion of workplace burnout."

To put it another way: carrying The Weight creates emotional exhaustion, which in turn leads to loneliness.

When we think about solving loneliness, we rush to amend the physical environment. We may invite a lonely friend out for a coffee, or take them for a night of dancing. And while camaraderie may help, it doesn't fix the root problem. When you consider emotional exhaustion as the main driver of loneliness, it's possible that time alone to rest and recharge may be the optimal solution at hand.

These findings have significant and far-reaching ramifications for head coaches, who live a lonely existence despite being around people sometimes as much as 14 or 15 or 16 hours per day. I attribute this to having company, but not connection.

Nobody to call

Justin Bieber almost didn't release his global top 20 hit "Lonely". He feared the humiliation he'd encounter for opening up and sharing his vulnerabilities. The song's lyrics deal with Bieber's agitation at having nowhere to turn in his decade as a global icon (it's easy to forget he's still only 26). Here are the lyrics from the first verse of the song:

> *Everybody knows my name now*
> *But somethin' 'bout it still feels strange*
> *Like lookin' in a mirror, tryna steady yourself*

And seein' somebody else
And everything is not the same now
It feels like all our lives have changed
Maybe when I'm older, it'll all calm down
But it's killin' me now
What if you had it all
But nobody to call?
Maybe then, you'd know me
'Cause I've had everything
But no one's listening
And that's just fuckin' lonely
I'm so lonely
Lonely

The song inadvertently describes the struggle head coaches deal with in private. In less than one hundred words, Bieber hits on many of the key elements of The Weight that we suppress and choose not to talk about: fame, identity, change, isolation, companionship, and feeling unheard.

There is also a key ponderance hidden in the middle of the verse: *Maybe when I'm older, it'll all calm down.* Failing to talk openly about these important issues is part of what hinders our progress on this topic. Let's agree to start to deal with this now, rather than waiting until we're older for it to calm down.

No one calls when you lose

Connacht Rugby head coach Andy Friend tells me that over the course of his coaching career he's picked up on a weird trend that can further entrench feelings of loneliness.

"When you win a game you hear from people you've never heard from before," he says matter-of-factly, "but when you lose a game, especially if you lose badly, you think your phone is broken because no one calls you."

Since Andy told me his theory, I've started testing it out on some of my coaching friends. One example stands out, where I text Melbourne Demons head coach Simon Goodwin and said "Andy Friend tells me no one texts you when you lose, just wanted to let you know I'm with you." Goodwin responded within minutes and said, "He's right. Thanks, Cody."

A slippery slope

For many head coaches, their success comes with haunting side effects. The emotional peaks and troughs, the constant over-stimulation, the irregular hours, the sleeplessness, the weight of caring, the self-criticism, the media criticism, the facade, the loneliness, the physical exhaustion, the stress of uncertainty, and lack of authenticity all combine to form a vicious tidal wave with devastating consequences. It becomes impossible to relax, and there are few places you can go or people you can turn to.

Many of us have not been equipped with the skills or emotional agility to deal with the groundswell of feelings that arrive like a cargo plane. For all of our progress on kindness and empathy, we must remember that outside of winning and losing big games, it's still socially unacceptable for us to cry.

One age-old coping mechanism is alcohol. It's baked into the fabric of society, a powerful bonding tool in sports, and a fantastic shortcut to relief. In some sports, like rugby, you could make the argument that 'having a beer' is so ingrained that it's a legitimate part of the game.

Former Dallas Stars head coach Jim Montgomery has only recently addressed his firing from the team, thanking Stars general manager Jim Nill for doing the right thing by cutting him loose. Montgomery told TSN, "I felt I was being a hypocrite. I was asking my players to do the right thing and yet I wasn't." Despite a 2008 DUI, numerous warnings from his wife, and additional warnings from Nill, Montgomery was unable to reign in his drinking habits.

Describing his alcoholism, Montgomery felt it was a progressive disease that hadn't impacted him in his 20s (he says he drank once per week) and 30s, but had gotten worse in his 40s. That's a plausible theory, but it's also worth noting that his struggles coincide with his rapid rise in coaching—it took Montgomery just eight years to advance from his first head coaching job in U20 hockey to the NHL.

The day he was let go by the Stars, Montgomery says he felt incredible shame and guilt. "I had to tell my wife and my children that I'd lost my job, not because the team was losing, but because of my own actions and addiction to alcohol," he professed.

Former USC Trojans football head coach Steve Sarkisian is another who has had a very public battle with alcoholism. After announcing that he and his wife were filing for divorce, Sarkisian was unceremoniously dumped by USC later that year after a string of alcohol-related incidents.

Sarkisian admitted that—only after watching SportsCenter's Scott Van Pelt praise New York Yankees pitcher CC Sabathia for seeking alcohol treatment—did he feel comfortable admitting he too needed help. "I thought to myself: 'Whoa, here's somebody who is like me, who is in a very high-profile position in sports and was being relatively commended or almost celebrated for going to do what he did," Sarkisian told CBS Sports.

While Montgomery is still out of the game and working daily on his 'conditioning', Sarkisian has found fierce advocates in Nick Saban and Dan Quinn, both of whom have shown compassion rather than condemnation. In Alabama and the Atlanta Falcons, Sarkisian has found not just positions that utilize his footballing nous, but also environments that set him up for success personally. Part of that belief from others stems from Sarkisian's refusal to shirk the issue himself, saying "It's a piece of me, this disease of alcoholism, but it doesn't define me. I have a lot more to offer than that."

We all need help

As I write this book, I am working with a therapist to help me reconstruct my relationship with alcohol. For most of my adult life, I've had a crippling belief that my friends think I'm boring, and don't really like me unless I'm drunk. It is a source of pride, not shame, that I reached out for help.

I don't have an addiction, and I'm not broken or weak. What I am, though, is a product of my environment. I come from a country that, outside of kangaroos and Crocodile Dundee, is best known for its drinking culture. It's so pronounced that my therapist, a Canadian, has a number of other Australian clients who all described similar fears of giving up drinking and the impact it would have on their closest friendships.

I've spent my life in sports teams where drinking is more so expected than it is encouraged. And I'm also from a generation of people taught to suppress their struggles, not speak up, and quietly turn to the bottle. I will not continue on that legacy.

Since retiring from my alcohol career, I've experienced extreme clarity of thought, enhanced emotional regulation, and my coaching delivery has improved. I have more time, more money, and more energy to take on projects that excite me.

This is not a sermon to implore you to quit drinking, but it is a call to action for you to consider whether drinking is working for you. If you want to make a change but feel stuck, I want you to know that it's not as bad as the picture you've painted in your head. It is scary for a while, but in my experience you will find support in unexpected places and guidance from unexpected people.

Jim and Steve: if you happen to read this, please feel free to get in touch with me. My email address is at the back of the book.

A weight off your shoulders

This chapter was as taxing to write as I'm sure it was to read. The truth is, though, that I've only just scratched the surface of covering all of the topics that could be helpful to modern head coaches.

Let's agree to move the ball forward by starting to talk about The Weight. Commit to having one conversation with a trusted friend. These small steps will begin to bring recognition to the challenges and normalize others to the topics at hand. Ironically, by talking about it, we also begin to lift some of the weight we've been carrying, which can only be a good thing.

Key Takeaways

1. Your fiercest rival isn't the opponent; it's yourself.

2. The emotional toll of head coaching is the largest barrier to your performance.

3. Even Hugh Jackman gets imposter syndrome. You should give yourself a break.

4. Our loneliness is fueled by emotional exhaustion. It's a vicious cycle that we must learn to manage better.

5. The answer is not at the bottom of a bottle.

*"No man knows who he truly is until
either his life is threatened or he's given power."*

Margaret Thatcher

You don't possess the God Particle

3

The giver of life

In 2012, physicists were able to confirm the existence of the Higgs boson, the so-called 'God Particle'. It was a monumental event for the scientific community, with the discovery holding the key to how galaxies, planets, and human beings are able to exist.

I'm not sure when, but somewhere along the line head coaches began acting like we, too, had found the God Particle, as if it was our presence that held the key to how our organization was able to exist.

With the growth in complexity in elite sports, this coach-centric mindset has fast become extinct, with the most sought-after coaches those who have been able to adapt to an ecosystem that they're not the center of. In this chapter, I'll explore how these coaches have navigated this transition and learned to let go.

Holding on too tight

The Collingwood Magpies are arguably the AFL's most storied franchise, featuring in forty-two Grand Finals in their 124-year history. A period of sustained success through the early 2000s garnered the club its fifteenth championship, before club legend Nathan Buckley took the reins as head coach and a sharp decline ensued.

Had Buckley not been a former captain and favorite son, it's unlikely he would have kept his job. The Magpies slipped down the ladder, finishing fourth, then sixth, before four consecutive seasons of missing the playoffs.

Buckley's obsessive drive as a player wasn't translating to success as a head coach. In fact, it was strangling him. "He'd want to know who was folding the towels," said a former staffer of Buckley's painful micromanagement during the club's lean years. It wasn't lost on the coach that he was holding on too tight, with Buckley reportedly telling the club's board that he fought himself every day to refrain from interfering with how staff were doing their jobs.

With his team in a tailspin and his job on the line, Buckley turned to yoga and relaxation in order to transform his natural tendency for tight control. The Nathan Buckley that emerged from an off-season retreat in Bali was drastically different in both demeanor and likability. The furrowed brow and gruff scowling persona were replaced by a smiling and jovial ray of light. Those outside the club noticed and appreciated the change, but long-time friends suggested this was the Nathan they'd known all along.

Buckley's personal transformation coincided with a reversal in form, with the Magpies jumping from thirteenth to third in just one season—an unprecedented leap in the AFL regular season. The team continued on, steamrolling the defending champion Richmond Tigers en route to a Grand Final appearance in 2018, where they would fall five points short of winning the ultimate prize. They have contended every season since.

Holding on for dear life

A poison chalice for leaders is hierarchical narcissism—the belief that once you've achieved a certain level in a hierarchy, that you cannot go back down the ladder. In some instances, it is valid, but often it is merely rabid ego fueling the fire.

On the flip side, examples abound of those who've created success by humbly assuming assistant coaching or support roles in order to keep learning their craft. One high-profile example is former England Rugby head coach Stuart Lancaster, who since 2016 has been 'senior coach' under Leo Cullen at Pro14 outfit Leinster.

"I'd coached international rugby and I walked into a provincial team where I was more experienced than the coaching staff that were there, but I didn't need to be front and center," Lancaster told me on an episode of *Where Others Won't*.

When I pressed him about the desire to strictly be a head coach, Lancaster said he believed at some point he'd probably want to be the boss again, but felt that he and Cullen complemented each other's strengths perfectly. He'd also done the sums, noting: "I'm 49 years old and I want to have a long-term career in coaching. When I look at some of the greats, they're at their best when they're 60. There's no age cap to coaching, so I want to keep getting better and learning."

Bayern Munich head coach Hansi Flick is another who put craft before ego after his dismissal from Hoffenheim (then in the German third tier) in 2005. Flick spent time as an assistant coach at Red Bull Salzburg and the German men's national team, winning the 2014 FIFA World Cup along the way.

Returning to club coaching in 2019, Flick initially joined Bayern as an assistant coach to new head coach Nico Kovač. Just four months into the post and with the team struggling, Kovač left Bayern and Flick assumed head coaching duties on an interim basis.

Having begun the season as the team's assistant coach and not been a head coach since 2005, Flick guided Bayern to just their second continental treble in the club's history, capturing the German Bundesliga, German Cup, and Champions League in his first season in charge.

You don't always need to be the boss. You can go back down the coaching hierarchy and continue to learn.

You can't do everything

Ben Olsen was Soccer America Player of the Year in 1997 and went on to earn 37 caps for the US men's national team. After spending the majority of his professional career playing for DC United in Major League Soccer (MLS), Olsen was thrust into the limelight just a couple of months after joining the team as an assistant coach.

Initially handed the team on an interim basis, six months later—at the age of 33—he became the full-time head coach. At the time, he was the youngest head coach in MLS history.

Olsen says while he had some leadership qualities as a player, that doesn't mean much when you walk into a room full of men and you're now the boss. Reflecting on those early days, he told me: "I had no coaching infrastructure, no idea who I was as a leader, and no idea how I wanted my team to play."

Figuring it out as he went, Olsen admits that he spent a lot of energy and toiled away for three or four years before he realized he had to start to let go. "There's too much going on now. There's too much information. Too many tools. As the head coach, you can't do it all," he told me.

While grateful for those early lessons, Olsen says he really started to advance in his craft when he realized he didn't possess the God Particle. "I needed to put some really sharp people around me that would hide my deficiencies. Once I started to figure out who I was, it was a really neat process to figure out who I needed to surround myself with."

You can't unlock everyone

Connacht Rugby head coach Andy Friend believes it's a fool's errand to think that you're the right coach for every one of your players. "The challenge of coaching," Friend told me, "is to try to unlock a massive array of personality types. We've got 43 players in our squad and the same key won't unlock every door."

Rather than quitting on a player if he's not the right coach, Friend prefers a more humble approach, utilizing the diversity within his staff to help develop the player. "I've got to understand that I'm not the right coach for that player. It's not a weakness to step back, it's a strength. Then I need to find who else within our staff can unlock that bloke," he told me during our conversation.

If the goal truly is to maximize the potential of every player, does it really matter if a strength coach or physio or assistant coach is the one that connects with them and unlocks their talent?

The Great Paradox of Coaching

The reason financial firms need to espouse 'integrity' as one of their cultural values is that the industry has scammed and swindled people for decades. Acting with integrity should be implicit when you handle the hard-earned money of millions of people. But unable to regulate their own behavior, they've had to make it explicit so there's a guardrail in place to protect them from themselves.

Coaching has its own variation of this, but it's not a word, it's a phrase: 'It's not about me'.

'It's not about me' is a necessary saying because of the rampant ego, narcissism, and selfishness that became commonplace through the professionalism of sports. While contemporary coaches are undoubtedly more player-centric than their predecessors, 'It's not about me' serves as our guardrail to not slip into the extremism of the past.

But here's the thing: 'It's not about me' is only a half-truth. It's well known in human behavior circles that people copy the behaviors of those they observe most, and in a sporting environment the person observed most closely is the head coach. So while 'It's not about me' may act as a convenient trigger for you to refocus your efforts on others, you must also remember that as a leader you create yourself in your team. (More about this in the next chapter.)

The Great Paradox of Coaching is that it is both not about you, and entirely about you.

Taking responsibility

It's relatively rare to hear a head coach take full responsibility for their team's performance, which is why it was so striking when Boston Celtics head coach Brad Stevens did it. After losing 4-1 to the Milwaukee Bucks in the 2019 NBA playoffs, Stevens refused to pass the blame.

"I did a bad job. As a coach, if your team doesn't find its best fit together, that's on you. So, I'll do a lot of deep dives on how I can be better."

Remember: as the head coach, it's both not about you, and entirely about you.

Dependent on your circumstances

When Luke Walton was fired as head coach of the Los Angeles Lakers, his former mentor, Golden State Warriors head coach Steve Kerr, gave an interesting interview. Asked his thoughts on Walton's firing, Kerr said:

> "I'm disappointed for Luke. In this job, you're 100% dependent on your circumstances—the strength of the organization, the momentum, the unity, everything has to be in good order. If it's not... there's going to be casualties and usually the coach is the first one.
>
> They're losing one of the best human beings in the NBA. They're losing a guy who knows the game as well as anybody I've ever met. They're losing someone who players believe in and want to play for.
>
> But again, he was dependent on circumstances, and I feel fortunate to have a set of circumstances here where we've got wonderful people stabilizing our organization every day. It doesn't happen often in the NBA."

As coaches, we like to think we're in control, but it's a mirage. Our success is largely dependent on our circumstances, so what's the point in giving yourself an ulcer from holding on too tight? You can care deeply and prepare ruthlessly while also acknowledging the whole thing is a best guess. It's not about you, and entirely about you.

Accepting randomness

Author Nassim Nicholas Taleb gave us a timeless reminder in *Fooled by Randomness*: "Nobody accepts randomness in his own success, only his failure."

A useful coaching shift

In his book *Shift Your Mind*, sport psychologist Brian Levenson explores the concept of polarity and how seemingly opposite traits appear in people at the same time. Levenson argues that the world's greatest performers switch mental states depending on whether they're preparing or performing. For instance:

- A world-class athlete flips between humble in preparation and arrogant during performance.

- The world's great entrepreneurs harness both fear and fearlessness to conquer the business world.

- Elite military units get uncomfortable in training so they can be comfortable during the mission.

These 'shifts' can be incredibly useful for coaches, too. Coaches must prepare humbly and diligently but show arrogance and adaptability during a performance. We must create environments so robust that we make ourselves redundant while simultaneously believing that we're the only person for the job. We need to be available and present for our teams, yet shift to being selfish about protecting time for our own self-care and development.

What Levenson hits on is the power of 'And'. For too long, we've been trying to assemble the perfect coach by focusing on their binary traits. We've been busy trying to suppress human traits like ego, rather than acknowledging the pattern of great coaches having both strong ego and strong humility. Rather than eliminating ego, we should be trying to master when to deploy it.

You might have read Ryan Holiday's *Ego Is The Enemy*; it was a motivational bestseller a few years back. Yet, despite the splashy title, ego is not the enemy. Rather, it is a useful human trait that, when used at the right time and in the correct context, can allow us to deliver when it counts. We don't need to choose between humility or ego, we need to learn how to harness humility 'and' ego.

A misnomer about self-awareness

To be able to shift between mindsets requires a lot of practice and self-awareness to be able to drive the right mindset when you need it. Like ego, though, there are many popular aphorisms about self-awareness that do more harm than good.

One such saying is: 'You must know yourself before you can know others'. It is a well-intentioned phrase that implores us to search out our inner being so we can in-turn learn about others. The problem is that it's not true.

Dr. Tasha Eurich, the world's leading expert on self-awareness, suggests that many of the popular catch cries about the subject are false when you challenge them with research. As it turns out, there are two sides to self-awareness—an internal side and an external side. It's possible for someone to be strong in one and not the other.

Dr. Eurich, who wrote the bestseller *Insight*, told me, "One of the truly surprising findings of our research was there's no relationship between the two types of self-knowledge." This means it's possible to be highly socially aware (knowing how you're perceived by others) while struggling to fathom your own sense of self.

Eurich's discovery is an important leap because it allows us to refocus on the non-linear nature of the pursuit of self-awareness, and acknowledge that the entry point may be a curiosity of others, not yourself.

It's their team

On February 12, 2018, the Golden State Warriors completely obliterated the Phoenix Suns in a mid-season NBA game. The 46-point winning margin was obscene, even for the Warriors who have reinvented what it means to be an offensive juggernaut in pro basketball. On an ordinary night, the winning margin would have been the headline story. But not this night.

At his postgame press conference, Golden State head coach Steve Kerr got vulnerable: "I have not reached my players for the last month. They're tired of my voice. I'm tired of my voice." Kerr's Warriors were coming off three successive NBA Finals appearances, amassing six months more basketball than teams like the Lakers and the Knicks, who hadn't made the playoffs over that same 3-year span.

"It's been a long haul these last few years. We just figured it was probably a good night to pull a trick out of the hat and do something different," Kerr added in an effort to punctuate his decision.

The story on this night was that Steve Kerr had allowed his players to coach themselves. Throughout the game, senior players took turns in drawing up plays on the whiteboard and presenting them to the team during timeouts. The coaching staff stood back, observing, but refusing to intervene.

Pressed further on why he had opted for the gimmick, Kerr launched into a magnificent explanation which ultimately slid under the radar amongst the kerfuffle:

"It's their team. I think that's one of the first things you have to consider as a coach; it's not your team. It's the players' team, and they have to take ownership of it. As coaches it's our job to nudge them, to guide them, but we don't control them. They determine their own fate."

Upon hearing Kerr's response, I had to rewind the video and listen again. In all my years around sport, I'd never heard a coach say anything like that before: *One of the first things you have to consider as a coach is it's not your team.*

It is a simple reminder worthy of a central place on any coaches' office desk or wall.

It's their game

The coach at the opposite end of the floor that night was Phoenix Suns head coach Jay Triano, so I called to hear his side of the story.

"Some people thought it was disrespectful, but Steve was good and came down to tell me that he didn't mean any disrespect. He told me that he considers it his players' team and he wanted them to own it," Triano recalled.

Rather than feeling aggrieved or disrespected, Triano loved the idea. "In an 82-game season, you're looking for any way to get your guys fired up. So, the next time we played the Warriors, which was about a month later, I told our guys that they were going to be coaching themselves," he explained.

Triano chose young veterans Troy Daniels and Devin Booker for coaching duties during the first timeout and gave them some pointers on some things they had to factor in: recognize the flow of the game, choose a play and diagram it, get all five guys on board, don't forget to think about substitutions.

"The buzzer went at the end of the timeout," according to Triano, "and Troy handed me back the clipboard with a smile on his face, and said: 'That was harder than I thought. Don't ask me to do that again.'"

Reflecting on it now, Triano says that he thinks giving meaningful control to the players, even in small doses, gives them a whole new level of respect for what you're going through as the coach. Perhaps even more powerful, though, is the reverse: the coaches' ability to have an unadulterated view into how the players are perceiving the game they're playing in.

Concluding, Triano added, "The players are the ones who have the best sense of whether the opposition has a weak defender or are cheating in their structures. As coaches, we better understand that what we're seeing on the sideline, the players are feeling on the court."

The true test of your coaching

Over a period of more than two years, Warriors head coach Steve Kerr was in searing pain. The cause: a botched surgery on his back— a battle wound from his long and successful playing career in the NBA.

Rather than struggle on like Doc Rivers, Kerr regularly took 'sick leave' from the team to rehabilitate his back. "They're better off without me, and I won't return until I can make them better," he is quoted as saying.

During the 2016 season, Kerr missed the first forty-three games of the season. Under assistant coach Luke Walton, the team went 39-4, and would go on to break the single-season record for wins before losing to Cleveland in the NBA Finals.

The following season, Kerr would again spend time away from the team, this time 'important' games. The coach missed three series of the playoffs (all 4-0 sweeps) and eventually returned for Game 2 of the NBA Finals—a rematch against Cleveland. In total, Kerr was away from the team for 46 days, with the Warriors not losing a game without him.

In two significant stints without their coach, the Golden State Warriors won fifty-one games and lost four. As Ken Blanchard, the godfather of situational leadership, says: "The true test of your leadership is not what happens when you're there, but what happens when you're not there."

More important than the wins was the fact that Warriors players witnessed their leader embody the values he espoused, removing himself from high-value situations for the betterment of the team. It's easy to say you're a values-led coach when it's benefiting your reputation, more difficult to uphold those values at the expense of accolades.

Bigger than the game

Leading 3-1 in the final game of the season, against one of the best teams in the league, San Diego Loyal players walked off the pitch. The move made headlines because teams that are winning don't often refuse to keep playing, but this was bigger than a game.

The week prior, Loyal player Elijah Martin had been the target of racist abuse, and his teammates were regretful that they didn't take a stand then and there. So when Collin Martin, who is gay, was the target of a homophobic slur, San Diego head coach Landon Donovan took action, facilitating his team's collective decision to refuse to play on.

"Our players, in the heat and passion of the moment, still wanted to play, but if we want to be true to who we are as a club, we have to speak and we have to act," Donovan said in a television interview. "After half-time we all decided if the player who used the homophobic slur was not removed from the game—either by the officials or by his coach—we would not play. If they are not willing to act, we have to act."

The offending player was not removed, so Donovan and his players didn't come out for the second half. The loss by forfeit cost San Diego a spot in the playoffs.

Had Landon Donovan's ego gotten in the way, he would have told the team to play out the half, wrap up their playoff spot, and deal with the misdemeanor later. Instead, he acted with purpose. This was bigger than him, and it was bigger than a game of soccer.

As it turns out, the clue was in their team name: Loyal.

Learning to let go

Just as the press conference was about to conclude, Nathan Buckley decided to speak out. "Can I just say something?" Buckley said, interrupting the silence. He had an ax to grind with the media.

"There was an article [about me] in the newspaper the other day, it was about emptiness," he began. The article had pointed out that Buckley had accumulated the most cumulative games as a player and coach in AFL history without winning a championship. "I just want to put on record my life is very far from empty. I don't have a championship but it's not going to define me whether I get one or not," Buckley added defiantly. "My life is very full. I've got a lot of love," he said, putting a stake in the ground.

I cannot think of another example from anywhere in the world where a head coach has so emphatically claimed their identity devoid of results. This was a coach who'd previously wanted to know which staff member was folding the towels in the locker room.

Rather than being just another snarky and egotistical head coach responding to media criticism, Buckley says he was triggered because it spoke to how he's been trying to help his players navigate the concepts of identity, success, and failure.

"To think that if you don't win a championship, that you're empty, is not consistent with my perspective on life," Buckley said when pressed by the journalist who'd written the article on why he'd responded the way he had. "One of my coaching philosophies is not so much an X or an O, but it's how we approach opportunities in the game, and how we accept winning and losing as part of the reality of what we do."

I believe Buckley's stance to be a watershed moment for head coaches everywhere. It's unprecedented for a coach in a billion-dollar industry to reclaim ownership of his self-worth and identity from outsiders. It's easy to get bullied into the same old narratives, but by owning his vulnerabilities and refusing to accept the standard terms and conditions, Nathan Buckley took away the bully's power. He also extinguished any remaining belief that it is he who possesses the God Particle.

Key Takeaways

1. Holding on tight doesn't make you less likely to lose your grip. It makes you unbearable to work with.

2. Accept that you can't do everything and you can't unlock everyone.

3. Head coaching is a paradox; it's simultaneously not about you and all about you.

4. Coaches create themselves in their teams. If your team mirrored your current behavior, who would they become?

5. It's possible to drop your ego and reinvent yourself while still working. Nathan Buckley has shown the way.

"At the end, I have to manage people, not players.
They are not players; they are people who play football.
I am not a manager, I am a man that works as a
manager. I think this is an important point."

Carlo Ancelotti

You're not
a coach

4

You're a person who coaches

"I knew I was gay, but I never allowed my players to know anything about me on a personal level," said former US women's national team soccer coach Jill Ellis.

Prior to winning 106 of her 132 games in charge of the national team, Ellis built UCLA's college program into a perennial winner, securing six-straight conference championships in the mid-2000s. It was at UCLA where Ellis grappled most with her identity. "It was still something that I was struggling with. I almost had two roles: I would stand up in front of my team as the head coach, but I'd also live in the shadows," she conceded. Ellis felt that as a college coach, coming out as gay would be used against her by opponents, particularly during the recruiting process.

It wasn't until Ellis and her partner Betsy decided to adopt a little girl that the idea of coming out began to crystalize. "When I held my daughter, I felt positive, and I didn't want this kid to live in the shadows. I wanted her to grow into a strong, independent woman and not have to deny who her parents were." After practice one day, Ellis decided to tell her team that she was gay, was adopting a child, and she and her partner planned to live as a family.

"Coming out was liberating, it just took this amazing amount of pressure off my shoulders," Ellis recalled vividly. Continuing, she added, "I've been blessed to coach the national team, and I couldn't have done that if I didn't decide to be true to myself. It was strengthening to me to know that you can have a career, be a strong female leader, and you can also be gay."

There are only two coaches in history to have won two soccer World Cups as a coach: Italy's Vittorio Pozzo in 1934 and 1938, and Jill Ellis in 2015 and 2019. Despite being one of the most decorated head coaches to ever grace planet earth, Ellis believes her most gratifying moment was sharing her true identity with her players. "When I became open about who I was, I found my purpose," she beamed.

This chapter looks at coaches who've taken different paths to find their identities, but who've ended up in similar places. By sharing their stories, they allow us to learn from their slip-ups and U-turns, as well as their triumphs.

Compassionate and strong

In a few short years, New Zealand prime minister Jacinda Ardern has become a beacon of modern leadership. Elected at the age of 37, Ardern has made the tiny island nation influential on a global scale with her powerful combination of humor, humility, and humanity.

Ardern, who gave birth to her first child while in office, has expertly led her country through the horrific mosque shootings at Christchurch, a volcanic eruption on the island of Whakaari, and the COVID-19 pandemic.

And yet, she's not been without doubters. "One of the criticisms I've faced over the years is that I'm not aggressive or assertive enough, or maybe somehow, because I'm empathetic, it means I'm weak," she's quoted as saying. "I totally rebel against that. I refuse to believe that you cannot be both compassionate and strong."

While remaining compassionate and strong, Ardern (at least outwardly) also maintains her charming comedic side. She makes funny Facebook videos, watches cheesy TV to unwind, and drove her electric Hyundai Ioniq to Auckland airport to pick up talk-show host Stephen Colbert.

What's most refreshing about Ardern, whom I consider to be a generational leadership talent, is the courage of her conviction.

Despite admitting to regular bouts of imposter syndrome, Ardern is steadfast in her belief in being as true as possible to who she is as a person, mother, leader, and Kiwi.

A natural creative

They say an artist paints his own reality, and the same can be said for a head coach.

In fact, for Ben Olsen, he quite literally paints his reality. In his youth, Olsen loved art class and spent his spare time designing sneakers. As a player, persistent ankle injuries helped reintroduce him to his creative streak, with his newfound love of painting helping him navigate two years of inactivity. Once he returned to regular playing time, though, Olsen shelved his paints, with the artistry of the game enough to satisfy his mind.

That changed again once he became a coach. "Most creatives will tell you that they can feel when they're being stifled and need to get creative energy out. When I started coaching, that outlet of playing the game was gone and it became harder to scratch my creative itch. So, I got on the paints again," he said with noticeable passion in his voice.

Painting isn't just a hobby to distract Olsen from his thoughts and anxieties, he's seriously talented. After setting himself up with a home studio, he now sells his pieces online at www.benolsen.art. "Once I got my studio and could focus on the art itself, I felt I really grew as a painter. I love it and it'll be something that I do for the rest of my life."

The most important role

Phoenix Mercury head coach Sandy Brondello has accomplished just about everything you can in basketball. A WNBA All-Star and four-time Olympian as a player, Brondello then led the Mercury to a championship in her first year as the team's head coach. Despite a dual role coaching the Australian national team and a husband who has coached primarily in Russia for the last decade, Brondello is very clear on her identity in life: "I'm a mother, number one. I love being a mom."

Rather than make (what would be justifiable) excuses about her packed schedule, Brondello takes her kids to school and their activities, and says she does most of her work at night after they're asleep.

A friend of mine has a saying: When you're clear who you are, you know what to do. Sandy Brondello is clear on who she is, and it guides everything she does.

Defined by coaching

Hue Jackson is a tortured man. The former Cleveland Browns and Oakland Raiders head coach owns the worst win ratio in NFL history: he went 3-36-1 over two-and-a-half seasons in Cleveland. After being fired by the Browns, he retreated to the guest room in his house, turned off the lights, and didn't come out for three days. "I could have laid there for months," Jackson said.

In his deep and disturbing portrait of Jackson, *Sports Illustrated* journalist Greg Bishop outlines why the coach was living in such torment:

> "Hue Jackson hurts this much because he defines himself first and foremost as a football coach, and the Browns decided they'd rather pay him to sit at home than to coach their team. He hurts because he is human, because there is a person behind all the memes, a man beyond the punchline, a proud and once-successful coach behind the laughingstock. Everyone knows why Jackson was fired—the losing is public, the record there to see. Few see the private pain."

In chapter two, I wrote about how workaholism was driving many head coaches into the ground, and Jackson is another who seems addicted to the grind that comes with life in the NFL. "He loves his wife and cherishes his children," Bishop wrote, "But football will always come first. Jackson buries his problems and ignores the toll exacted by his job."

Jackson took Cleveland's losing so personally that he says it's what will be written on his tombstone. In fact, emergency surgery was all that saved him from having a tombstone after he returned dizzy and out of breath from a morning run. He blames his fully-blocked artery on genetics rather than his haunting obsession with football, a notion his wife is less convinced about.

Few question whether Hue Jackson is a good coach, he is. But at what cost? Is it worth missing 95% of your daughters' lives for the sake of righting a win-loss record that you think is unfairly skewed? Only Hue Jackson can determine that, and only you can determine what's right for you. I'm just not sure that having your win-loss record on your tombstone is indicative of a full life that's been well-lived. 'Father, husband, and football coach' sounds much nicer.

"I realized I was a better husband and father"

During the COVID-19 lockdown, something occurred to Connacht head coach Andy Friend. "With the extra time available, I realized how much better of a husband and father I was," he told me. When his team returned to play, Friend decided to make changes rather than merely slip back into the ways of the past.

"I used to call every single player on team selection day and have a detailed conversation with them about whether they'd made the team," he outlined to me on the phone. "I'd arrive home that night with a throbbing headache and collapse on the couch. But I wanted to be able to get home and cook for my wife, spend time with her, and talk to my kids. So I changed how we did selection."

Friend acknowledged that he was making it hard for himself by making it easy for the players, so he drew up a proposal and took it to his leadership group for discussion.

Now Connacht's team selection is disseminated differently, and there's still time allocated for those players who want a detailed discussion with the coach. More pertinent is that Friend is also able to feel more accomplished in his two most important roles in life: as a husband and a father.

Create yourself, continuously

One of the mistakes we make when discussing identity is talking about it as a stagnant thing. In reality, we have many identities, all of which are in motion, none of which are set.

As physics icon Richard Feynman once said: "You are under no obligation to remain the same person you were a year ago, a month ago, or even a day ago. You are here to create yourself, continuously."

Dress to ~~impress~~ be yourself

One of my recent projects was to clean up my photo albums and consolidate them in one place. Looking back on twenty-something years of photos, one consistent thought crossed my mind: 'What the hell was I wearing?'

It got me thinking.

Coachwear isn't often something that springs to mind as a consideration when you're talking about identity, but as an outward manifestation of your personality, it's worthwhile spending some time reflecting on. And that's the thing with me looking back on my old photos; what I was wearing was a depiction of who I was at that time in my life. My backward-looking disdain doesn't matter so much as me being comfortable in those clothes at the time the photo was taken.

Recently, I watched a Premier League game where Fulham head coach Scott Parker wore a three-piece suit with a tie pin, and Sheffield United head coach Chris Wilder wore his team tracksuit with bright white sneakers. The contrast couldn't have been more pronounced, but both men owned their distinct looks.

"I think the best-dressed coach is Pep Guardiola," Liverpool head coach Jürgen Klopp said recently. "Everything Pep wears looks exactly right for him. He doesn't wear a suit, just casual stuff."

Klopp says that early in his coaching career he was so engrossed in the game that he didn't even think about how he looked. It was when he arrived at Borussia Dortmund, a giant of German club football, that he began to think about his look. "I went for a while wearing jeans and a shirt. But I just didn't feel comfortable," he mused. "Be yourself as a coach," Klopp advised, adding, "If you want to look great, then wonderful!"

(Personally, I am a fan of the relaxed workman look John Herdman rocked while coaching Canada during the FIFA Women's World Cup. A crisp white shirt, open at the neck, with sleeves rolled up; it's a statement unto itself.)

Who you are impacts those you coach

Many forget the great strides taken by Liverpool under Jürgen Klopp's predecessor, Brendan Rodgers. The Northern Irishman took the Reds to within a whisker of winning the Premier League title in 2014, and also signed players that would prove pivotal to Klopp's team that would go on to win domestic, continental, and world championships.

Profiled in a chapter of Michael Calvin's sensational book *Living On The Volcano*, Rodgers described how he views himself and how he tries to interact with his players. "I don't see myself as a coach, I see myself as a welfare officer," he began. "I look after the needs of the player. I work with these kids like they're my own. I give them advice like I was giving advice to my son." Expanding on that, Rodgers articulated that player welfare requires more than acknowledging their technical, tactical, physical, and mental wellbeing; it includes looking at their social lives and environment as well.

Mario Balotelli was widely regarded as Rodgers' worst signing at Liverpool, with the striker contributing only four goals in his year at the club. Nonetheless, Rodgers recognizes that Balotelli's human circumstances make him a unique proposition to work with. "Mario's starting point is different from most others. Not too many were born into a family of four and were the only one given away for adoption, so you can't treat him like everybody else. You can't treat him like the guy who has grown up in a secure family."

To outsiders, Mario Balotelli remains a frustrating enigma who has failed to fulfill his immense talent, but viewed through Rodgers' welfare prism, he's a young man who has endured unspeakable trauma and is struggling to understand his place in the world. In the coaching community, Mario Balotelli would be dismissed as being difficult and uncoachable, which only serves to deepen his feeling of being an outsider.

We should also interrogate our own beliefs about 'coachability' and ask ourselves why it is we shy away from difficult players. It is my belief that we seek out coachable players because it's easy on us as coaches. If everyone acts the same and doesn't think for themselves (ie., stripping away their identity), we're not forced to have any sort of intellectual or emotional agility. It is the definition of the 'do as I say, not as I do' method of coaching.

To have coachability, you need coach ability. Rather than asking whether every player is coachable, perhaps we should ask whether we have the strength of identity to be able to coach different types of players.

You create yourself in your team

Jürgen Klopp's Liverpool team is undoubtedly created in his image. In a newspaper interview, assistant coach Pep Lijnders described Klopp as "the leader and face of the team, the one who defines the character and who stimulates everyone."

Klopp's intense excitement and unwavering belief in others have become hallmarks of his Liverpool side, who have been almost unbeatable in both English and European soccer for two seasons. Klopp has succeeded in creating an environment emblematic of himself, namely his energetic and intense personality is replicated in the team's defensive system, known as the counterpress.

As Lijnders explains, "The heart of the team is the heart of the coach. The character of the coach will become the character of the team in the long term, because there is no stronger weapon than your own example."

If you're ever curious about what it is you believe the world to be, take a step back and observe your team and how they show up. Whether consciously or unconsciously, coaches create themselves in their teams.

Who are you as a coach?

Another prevalent coach who has created a team in his image is Golden State Warriors head coach Steve Kerr, but that image wasn't always clear to him. Before his first season as head coach, Kerr arranged a visit with Pete Carroll and the Seattle Seahawks. After day three of the visit, the two coaches sat together in Carroll's office.

"How are you going to coach your team?" Carroll probed. Kerr, slightly bewildered, thought they were about to engage in a conversation about tactics and responded, "You mean, like, what offense are we going to run?"

Carroll rebuffed, "No, no. That stuff doesn't matter."

A consistency that Carroll had noticed over 40 years in football was that the head coaches who'd achieved influence and longevity had an inherent understanding for who they were as people—their uniqueness, their personal values, and their uncompromising principles. On an episode of *Flying Coach*, the podcast Kerr and Carroll started together, Carroll explained in more detail what he meant that day in his office:

> "What I wanted to get you to start to think about was, Who are you as a coach? What are you going to stand by? What do you stand for? All of those things are going to come into play because you're going to be in training camp and some guy is not going to show up for a meeting.
>
> Then he's going to be late for the bus. Then he's going to spout off at one of your players during a game. There are all these things that are going to happen: How are you going to react to them? It has nothing to do with X's and O's.
>
> Every time you deal with a situation you're making a statement about who you are, and then the players are going to watch you. Do you believe in something or are you just dealing with things randomly? In my opinion, that's the really cool stuff about figuring out how to coach."

Carroll sent Kerr back to the hotel with some homework: sit down and make a list of your top ten values. Those ten values were eventually whittled down to four, which were infused into the daily habits and routines of the Warriors, as well as acting as Steve Kerr's north star for everything he does as a coach.

Steve Kerr's coaching values

Joy: inject fun and laughter into practice every day.

Mindfulness: being aware of what's going on around you.

Compassion: to understand each person's circumstances—their life, their motivators, and their unique challenges.

Competition: we want to keep score of everything.

There are three questions at hand for any head coach: Do you know what your values are? Are they genuinely yours? And, do you adhere to them or just use them to instruct others?

It works the other way around, too

Ole Gunnar Solskjær's nine-month stint as head coach of Cardiff City was a torrid affair. "I got an offer from Cardiff and I jumped on it. But the situation didn't suit me. The style of play that I wanted to play didn't suit the players," he said in an interview with Damien Hughes and Jake Humphrey.

After racking up trophies as coach of Molde FK in his native Norway, Solskjær fell into the trap of thinking the coaching game was easy. In hindsight, he admits that he was too stubborn when he took the Cardiff job; he thought he'd have success with relative ease. Having played the majority of his career under Sir Alex Ferguson at Manchester United, Solskjær had firmly held beliefs about how a team should play. Serial winning as a player and coach had validated his philosophy, but had also rendered him inflexible. After just nine wins in nine months, Solskjær was sacked from Cardiff City.

Reflecting back, Solskjær recognized where he went wrong: he wasn't being himself. "I realized that my persona at Cardiff wasn't me. I said I was open and honest and my door was always open for the players, but I was still a little bit too distant. I didn't get the relationship I wanted with the players."

Solskjær's self-diagnosis pointed him to the realization that both his personal identity and coaching identity were askew. By rigidly imposing a style of play and being remote personally, he created an environment that was rigid and closed off—not signals we typically associate as conducive to high-performance.

Psychologically Informed Environments

It's easy to fall out of sync with who you are. As human beings, we're messy. We're forgetful. We're both rational and irrational. We have little control over our mood. Our feelings come and go without warning. And, like Ole Gunnar Solskjær, we say we're open and honest when we're not.

Sport psychologist Dan Abrahams, who has worked with the likes of AFC Bournemouth and England Rugby, explains our messiness like this: "Humans are a cocktail of cognitions, emotions, motivations and behaviors interacting. And here's the thing: these driving forces interact in parallel rather than serially. Thoughts, feelings, and motivational urges emerge together rather than in sequence."

To recognize the messiness of people, Abrahams suggests we create Psychologically Informed Environments (PIEs) for our teams. What does this mean, exactly? "It means taking into account the psychological make-up of our people, and factoring their emotions, thinking, personalities, experiences, cultures, and values into our decision-making."

Admittedly, this is a new realm for coaches, who've been brought up thinking behavioral uniformity is the best way to create team success. But if we want to consider ourselves experts in behavior change, we first must become experts in the human condition. And that means learning to be comfortable with the messiness.

It's not just about authenticity

Abrahams says that being an elite-level leader isn't just about being authentic, it's about being a great performer. He writes, "A high-performing personality in sport is a mix of authentic and inauthentic. It's about knowing yourself and doing what you do in the way you best do it. But it's also knowing what you're not good at and filling the missing gaps by being a great actor. Ultimately, performance can just be an act."

In seeking to explore your own identity, the task at hand is not to find pure authenticity, it's to amplify your impact by knowing when you need to act. Learning to find the balance between the two is difficult, but walk down the path anyway. The worst thing that can happen is you begin to understand yourself a bit better.

Finding your own tendencies

In the early days of Ben Olsen's coaching career, a sport psychologist had him take the Myers-Briggs personality test. With results in hand, the psychologist marched into the office and taped Olsen's chart, alongside two others, to the wall. What Olsen noticed immediately was that his profile lay in stark contrast to the other two emblazoned on the wall. "Whose are they?" he asked. "This one is Bruce Arena, and this one is Bob Bradley," the psychologist responded.

"The two greatest coaches in US men's soccer history," laughed Olsen as he retold the story to me, adding: "The psychologist said to me 'Listen, this is going to be a very, very tough job for you. You can do it, but it's going to be extremely taxing for your personality type.'"

Still feeling bulletproof after his successful playing career, Olsen didn't understand or agree with the assessment. "I appreciated his honesty, but at the time I wish he would've sugar coated it a little bit more for me," Olsen admitted.

Looking back now, he says the analysis was pretty spot-on and that throughout his decade at the helm of DC United, he found navigating the ups and downs of being a head coach to be emotionally exhausting for him. "Some coaches are capable of dealing with the natural volatilities of a season without any ill effects. That was the point he was making by showing me Bob's and Bruce's profiles. I'm not one of those coaches," he said with sharp conviction.

Information is power, and despite not being entirely suited to life as a coach, Olsen was armed with what would perhaps become the single most important nugget that would fuel his prolonged success: the power to choose when to be authentic, and when to act.

The user manual to me

Nancy Spotton is a hugger. Whether you're a lifelong friend or meeting her for the first time, you won't escape an encounter without a big meaningful hug.

I let Nancy know that I was curious to learn more about my leadership tendencies. She invited me to try the TAIS psychological tool that her company, MPWR Performance, uses to help build self-aware leaders.

After taking the assessment (and collecting my hug), Nancy walked me through my profile in granular detail, allowing me to see my tendencies as a leader and a person. Here's what I found out about myself:

- I have high awareness, am a deep thinker and am highly analytical.

- I prefer to solve complex problems by immediately getting to the root cause.

- I enjoy one-on-one conversations with intelligent people, but find gossip and frivolous conversations agonizing.

- I'm perceived as aloof because I'm introverted and go inside my own head for comfort.

- I read rooms effectively and my high awareness is constantly scanning for body language, expressions, music, voice cadence, the shape of people's eyebrows. This digestion of information becomes exhausting, and I'm not at my best when I'm tired.

- I have low-action focus, which means I barely remember what I had for breakfast.

- I am a rule follower rather than a risk taker (one area I disagree with the test).

- I'm dependable, but very black and white.

- I am a leader who will be the first to stand up and want to lead in a group situation. I lead by letting others make their own decisions, and by modeling the way rather than micromanaging.

All-in-all, I found the personality assessment helpful in identifying characteristics that I already knew I had. It was a worthwhile secondary validation. Seeing myself charted out against other leaders was informative and helped reinforce that, despite my flaws, I'm not all that crazy (or perhaps we're all crazy).

Small changes

Now armed with a dossier of my own tendencies, I was able to reflect on changes I could make that would take my coaching to the next level. Here are five of those changes:

1. Add detail-oriented people to my coaching staff.

2. Reiterate our culture of psychological safety by imploring others to speak up when I'm forgetting a key detail.

3. Begin to vocalize what I believe the root cause of an issue to be so that others can help co-create a solution faster.

4. Interrupt myself when I'm beginning to retreat into my own head for comfort.

5. Smile more (I didn't need a test to know this one).

Strength & conditioning

Like anything else in the performance world, the success of psychological profiling isn't in the assessment itself, it's what you do with the findings. Used effectively, your psychological profile can become the catalyst for in-depth and meaningful conversations with those in your environment. The ability to show others your assessment allows you to co-create relationships of understanding and acceptance and speak to your deficiencies from a place of strength, rather than shame.

While tests like Myers-Briggs or TAIS can give you a great baseline for understanding your personal tendencies, it's important to remember that the report isn't actually who you are. My test will tell you that I probably won't remember your birthday and that I'm introspective, but it won't tell you that I'm the son of a single mother. That fact alone may be the single most important thing you can know about me.

Here's why: My concept of hard work was shaped by observing my mother become one of the top salespeople in her industry despite being orphaned at age 16 and never finishing high school. I didn't realize this until I was older, but many of our 'family vacations' were really just Mom's work trips; we took her company car and stayed in cheap motels so she could expense the cost back to her employer.

My social conditioning can tell you just as much, if not more, about my work than the test data can.

You are a performance multiplier (for yourself)

A new level of performance awaits the coach who is willing to apply the magnifying glass to themselves, peel back the layers of their own identity, and begin to approach themselves with curiosity rather than condemnation.

Key Takeaways

1. You're not a coach; you're a person who coaches.

2. Your team is a mirror to who you are as a person—both good and bad.

3. You don't have one identity, you have multiple intermingled personalities that are always evolving. Your most important identities relate to your family, not your sport.

4. An easy way to begin to learn about who you are is by taking a psychological assessment.

5. Remember: a psychological assessment isn't who you are, it merely serves as the foundational learnings about your tendencies.

"The more you learn about how your brain works, the better your chances of using it most efficiently, optimizing your intellectual capabilities, and accomplishing even more in life than many people who may score higher than you on standardized intelligence tests."

Richard Restak

You're hired
for your brain

5

Shortcuts

Did you know that the human brain is not designed for thinking? Quite the opposite, actually; it's designed for taking shortcuts.

As renowned psychologist Dr. Lisa Feldman Barrett explains, "Even when your brain does produce conscious thoughts and feelings, they are more in service to the needs of managing your body than you realize."

At any given time, your brain is attempting to predict your needs, taking shortcuts based on signals it picks up from a whole range of environmental and physiological sources. To illustrate this point, Feldman Barrett uses the example of what happens when you're thirsty. "Water takes about 20 minutes to reach your bloodstream, but you feel less thirsty within mere seconds. What relieves your thirst so quickly? Your brain does."

Using your past experience of drinking water as a signal, your brain quenches your thirst long before the water has a physiological impact on your body. Rather than wait the full 20 minutes, your brain takes a calculated shortcut and moves on to trying to predict what you'll need next.

Recently, I sat near my television while The Fireplace Channel played. As the artificial fire crackled and hissed, I felt a warm sensation on the side of my face closest to the 'fire'. Just like with drinking water, my brain was using my past experiences with sitting by a fire to simulate warmth on my skin, but also warning me not to get too close.

So why is this important for coaches? When we understand our design flaws, we can begin to purposefully rewire ourselves to reach all-new levels of performance. To start, we must first acknowledge our base brain state, otherwise we're more prone to... You guessed it; take shortcuts.

Knowledge work

In his 1959 book, *The Landmarks of Tomorrow*, management thinker Peter Drucker introduced the term 'knowledge work' to the popular lexicon. Shortly after, he began writing about 'knowledge workers', who he argued were different from clerical, white-collar workers who performed repetitive tasks; who in-turn were different from blue-collar workers who did physical labor.

The key to knowledge workers, Drucker suggested, was their ability to use convergent and divergent thinking to solve problems. In essence, Drucker was describing the modern office employee— the analyst, the designer, the marketer—whose creativity, pattern recognition, intellectual reasoning, and general knowledge are used to expand the resources available to an organization.

Reading this, I'm sure you can see immediate similarities with the work you do as a coach, but I would argue that knowledge work has another gear, and us coaches are in a different echelon altogether.

High-performance knowledge work

My proposition is that head coaching in elite sport is, in fact, high-performance knowledge work. The traditional models used to problem solve in a knowledge work environment are essentially null and void when stress-tested in an elite sporting context.

In traditional office work, convergent and divergent thinking plays out on a delayed time scale, whereas a coach's knowledge work plays out in real-time (and in the public domain). In coaching, the complexity of the patterns, the intensity and pressure of decision-making, and the demands placed on one's cognitive resources all require preparation of the highest caliber. It is this requirement for training and reconfiguration of the brain's base state that truly differentiates the high-performance knowledge worker from the modern office worker that Drucker was describing. This is an entirely new level of operation.

A stark reality, though, is that many head coaches aren't ready for this heightened level of preparation. Despite knowing many of the cutting edge secrets to human performance, we pass them on to our players and follow none of them for ourselves. This chapter puts many of our coaching behaviors under a microscope and argues that the head coach of the future will prepare themselves for performance just as robustly as we ask our players to.

We, the decision makers

In his book, *Entrepreneurial Leadership*, JetBlue chairman Joel Peterson suggests that great leaders should be making only the difficult 51-49 decisions. His rationale is that someone else should be making the more-obvious 70-30 decisions. If you're hoarding the easier decisions it creates unnecessary friction and breeds distrust.

While necessary for great leadership, it's exhausting making frequent borderline decisions. In chapter two, I outlined how coaches are already living in a state of depletion that is not conducive to strong decision-making. But there are things we have control over which can set us up to best wrestle with the 51-49 decisions that come our way.

Our job is to notice things, point them out to others, and make wise choices based on what we've seen. It sounds simple, but to perform them in real-time requires cognitive capacity and alertness. And, as with our players' physical performance, there is literature to support the fact that there are steps we can take that will result in increased performance if we prepare properly.

The biggest barrier to advancement? We, the coaches. It is our mentality, and being stuck in 'service mode', which has stymied our belief that we're worthy of living in a state of optimization.

It's okay to think of yourself as an asset

To keep himself in shape, Milwaukee Bucks head coach Mike Budenholzer spends as much time as he can in the weight room. Not only are there obvious physical benefits, but he also suggests it helps him connect with the sports medicine staff in a more personal way. "I do better in-season because I'm around guys that are working out, the weight room, the training staff," he told journalist Dan Woike. "You don't want to overwork them. The most important guys aren't us," said Budenholzer.

While performance departments are overworked and under-resourced across the sporting landscape, and professional athletes are certainly the stars of the show, it is on us as coaches to stop saying things like, "The most important guys aren't us."

You can still lead with humility while being confident in the value you bring. You can still serve others and selfishly protect time for your own performance. The game is for the players, but their ability to perform relies on your ability to perform. Head coaches are substantial assets and a crucial piece of the leadership puzzle. It's okay for us to admit that.

The lessons are right there...

In their book *The Process*, performance coaches Fergus Connolly and Cameron Josse present the Four-Coactive Model for Player Preparation. In explaining how cognition factors into a player's psychological development, they write:

> "The ability to focus and learn is profoundly impacted by stress and disruption to basic health. Being capable of engaging fully on the practice field, in the film room, or during supplemental learning scenarios, and transferring these experiences to long-term memory, is inextricably linked to a player's overall wellbeing."

Why would it be any different for a head coach?

A culture of napping

"The Army has always had an internal dynamic that real men don't need sleep and can just push on, and it's incredibly stupid." That's Lt. Gen. David Barno, who was commander of combined forces in Afghanistan from 2003 to 2005.

Being interviewed by the *New York Times* about the Army's new Holistic Health and Fitness manual, Barno is as clear in his thinking as someone with a healthy eight hours of sleep: "Combat is a thinking man's business and your brain doesn't function without sleep," he added.

Traditionally, the United States' military fitness guidelines were focused entirely on physical health, but as the fatigue-based errors have piled up and the science has changed, modern upgrades were needed. The manual now includes suggestions on spirituality and recognizing the interconnectedness of all people and things, as well as guidance on when to take short naps versus long naps.

Masking chronic exhaustion under the guise of 'toughness' was found to be a significant factor in four Navy accidents, including one that left 17 sailors dead when a high-tech destroyer collided with a slow-moving, easy-to-see cargo ship near Tokyo. A 2016 article on the Army's own website titled "The science behind why you should stop chugging so many energy drinks" had warned of a concerning trend of service members' over-reliance on caffeinated drinks to stay awake and feel alert.

"It's a trend in sports, too, to use stimulants to compensate for sleep deprivation," remarked Dr. Meeta Singh, a sleep expert who consults teams like the Washington Nationals, Los Angeles Lakers, New Orleans Saints, and the Belgian men's soccer team. Dr. Singh points out that while caffeine stimulates alertness, it doesn't impact the part of the brain responsible for decision-making. In other words, energy drinks will keep you alert, but they won't put you in a state to make stronger decisions.

For the Army, writing nap time into official guidelines is a huge leap forward, but its success relies on modeling from higher-ups. General Barno admits that he worked hard to protect his full sleep quota and says that it gave him the advantage of a clear head while in a high stakes environment.

They used to say that real men don't need sleep. Now real men go for a nap whenever they can.

A clear mind

Carly Clarke is the head coach of Ryerson University's women's basketball program, where she guided the Rams to a national championship final in 2016. It was the first national title game the school had ever appeared in, in any sport. Clarke has also coached multiple Canadian age-group national teams to medal performances at FIBA tournaments.

"As I reflect on big moments or big games that I've been a part of, I think I've had the clearest mind because the preparation and planning and direction have been sorted out in advance," she told me. Part of that preparation, she says, is making sure she's had enough sleep beforehand.

A meticulous planner, Clarke adds: "I know sleep is important to being great in big moments. It doesn't take away all of the anxiety and worry, but it certainly helps you have a clearer mind and make faster decisions, which are what's needed in big games."

Sleep is your save button

"Throughout the day you take in all sorts of information, but you only hit the save button when you're asleep," Dr. Singh told me during our fascinating conversation. "It's not just a bulk save," she continued, "A sign of a good memory is the ability to forget unnecessary information and store what's useful. That pruning is a function of deep sleep, which is a rarity for coaches at the professional level."

Put simply: we don't get smarter because of what we do during the day, we get smarter because of how well we sleep at night.

Dr. Singh helps teams plan for hectic schedules and prepare for the ramifications of poor sleep and insomnia. Often though, her work starts and stops with the players and does not extend to the coaches or other staff.

Poor sleep habits have obvious side effects for athletic workers, but it is perhaps more detrimental to the executive functioning and higher levels of thinking required of the head coach. Sleep deprivation impacts your concentration, attention, ability to shut out distraction, and flexibility of thought. In addition, the ability to put previously-stored information together and come up with novel solutions is affected.

Lack of sleep also creates problems with emotional regulation, which can color how you take in information, interrupt how you communicate with your players and staff, and how you give or receive feedback. Studies have also shown that poor sleep impacts your self-awareness, a trait most coaches would agree is central to their success.

Dr. Singh says that you don't need to listen to her, but being chronically sleep deprived is like being drunk, and when someone's had five beers, they're usually not the best judge of whether they should drive home. "We always talk about getting a competitive advantage, so why don't we get that edge by having a good night's sleep?" she added in summation.

A finite resource

Dr. Amy Kruse is world-reknowned for her seminal research into neuroplasticity. While working at DARPA, the US military's high-performance research arm, Kruse discovered that by mirroring the brainwaves of expert marksmen, it's possible to dramatically accelerate and ultimately enhance a novice sniper's performance. Kruse's work has all sorts of applications for military operatives, like repeated skill execution and fast-tracking the ability to learn languages, but it also has civilian applications that coaches can learn from.

"One of the interesting things that neuroscience has taught us is that decision-making is a finite resource. You can't just will yourself to make better decisions. For head coaches, who are tasked with rapid decision-making for prolonged periods, we know that it is incredibly depleting, both in terms of your cognitive resources and your attentional capacity," Kruse told me, before adding, "And that's before we add the emotional complexity of making those decisions in front of 40,000 screaming fans, night after night."

While Kruse's work is incredibly complex, her solutions are

refreshingly simple. Suggestion one is to invest in sleep: "If you only have two nickels to rub together, spend them both on sleep. It has the most bang for buck in terms of brain health and decision-making," she declared.

Suggestion two, Kruse says, is to explore mindfulness and meditation. "One of the reasons they're so beneficial is they teach you to focus your attention. When you force the brain to jump around and focus on too many things, you lose the ability to have sustained attention when it matters most."

A game-time decision

At around 2 PM on an NBA game day, players go for their naps. It's such a well-known practice that league and union officials know not to call the players in the mid-afternoon because they'll be asleep.

The theory goes that with a pregame restorative nap, the players will be sharp, alert, and close enough to their physical peak for tipoff. So what do the coaches do while the players are in bed? They work. Some last-minute scheming. A local media interview. Planning for tomorrow's game.

As Dr. Kruse has already pointed out, decision-making is a finite capacity. It also declines throughout the day. "If I knew that I had to be on my A-game at 7 PM, I'd change everything about how I spent my day," she explained conclusively. "Every decision would be made for me that day; my clothes would be laid out and my food would be chosen for me. I wouldn't make a decision at all. I'd save up all my capacity for the game."

Since coaches are susceptible to the same performance impediments as players, like pregame stress, travel fatigue, strange environments, and postgame hyper-arousal, both Dr. Kruse and Dr. Singh agreed that, where possible, coaches should look at adopting similar napping protocols to their players.

Eating yourself silly

"The majority of coaches have very poor nutritional habits, and it's pretty obvious when you see the physical shape that most of them are in," said Pratik Patel, who spent three-and-a-half years as the director of performance nutrition for the New York Giants.

To cope with the extreme demands of the job and help manage The Weight, Patel says many coaches turn to vices like alcohol and comfort food. "A head coach needs to be focused, energized, and able to make quick and rational decisions. The issue is that unhealthy behaviors like lack of sleep and excessive energy intake can directly and negatively impact health and cognitive performance," Patel cautioned.

Patel believes that poor nutrition hurts coaches more than they realize, and sees the whole situation as a missed opportunity, especially for performance experts. He told me: "It's such a funny thing when you think of it. Some coaches will go to such great lengths to try to gain an advantage on their opponent, but they overlook that taking care of themselves is one of the best ways to do that. We spend so much time and energy learning about performance and health, but most outside of the players rarely take their own advice or practice what they preach."

While quick to point out that there is no one-size-fits-all solution to coach nutrition, Patel does have some advice on how to think about solving the issue. "Each person's individual health and situation is going to be completely different," he prescribed, adding: "Just handing coaches a 'nutrition plan' won't do any good because their days are so volatile. But it would help for someone to make decisions for them, so they don't need to think about what to eat or where their next meal or snack is coming from."

Patel is right. Meal preparation or nutrition planning is a small change that any coach can make, and the evidence suggests it can have a substantial impact on cognitive capacity and alertness. You'd kick yourself if your penchant for the McDonald's drive-thru was the reason you made a crucial coaching error in the final seconds of the big game.

Out for a run

For a long time, I felt guilty for not having a meditation practice. I had tried a bunch of different techniques that were suggested by colleagues, but none of them had worked for me.

Then, a friend asked me something that made me realize I'd

actually had a meditation practice all along. In a casual conversation, they asked, "What do you think about when you go on your long runs?"

Unbeknown to me, I'd been engaging in active meditation the whole time. I typically run six to eight kilometers, five times a week, and use that time to drift into my subconscious mind. Long-distance runners often describe the time alone out on the road as some of their most valuable thinking time, but it had never occurred to me that this was a form of meditation.

More recently, I've been setting off without a defined destination, forcing me to listen to my body intently so that I have enough energy to get home. It doesn't allow for the same deep introspection, but does allow you to get into a meditative state.

What gets your attention, gets your time

You may be sitting reading this book thinking, 'I know all of this, but I don't have time to implement any of these changes'. But here's the thing: you do have the time, you're just choosing to spend it elsewhere.

George Washington University's Jamion Christian is one of the most exciting young coaches in college basketball, with both ESPN and *The Athletic* naming him to their 40-under-40 lists in 2020.

Christian is a long-time devotee of meditation, a practice he told me he's been exposed to for most of his life, with his father being an Olympic-caliber track and field athlete. What's striking about Christian's meditation practice is two things: it's a team-wide activity, and he's configured gameday around it.

When I asked him for specifics, Christian enthusiastically outlined how he gets himself ready to perform. "I get to the arena before anybody else, and I go and sit in the very top row. I listen to the popcorn being made, the people coming into the stadium. I want to feel the energy in the building," he explained. "Our players will feel the energy in the building, so I want to be aware of it and in-tune with it so that I can coach them properly." Christian says that most of the time the pregame energy is similar, but sometimes he can feel when the fans are nervous and don't believe his Colonials can win.

After preparing the team and sending them out onto the floor,

Christian stays in the locker room to meditate again. "The players have to be on the court 10 minutes before tipoff, so I usually meditate from game minus-8 to game minus-5. That last three minutes is about putting myself in a place that I can be ready for whatever happens. We plan a lot and we train a lot, but you don't really have control over what's going to happen. I think that's hard for people to understand, but that's a reality," he told me.

For most coaches, the minutes leading up to game-time is filled with worry and anxiety. They're thinking about everything that could go wrong, hoping the opposition's star player has an off night. Not Christian. "For those last three minutes, it's all about gratitude. I think about my son, his birth, holding him, the love I have for him, and the love I have for my wife," he said with a smile on his face, as if he was picturing his family as he talked to me. Christian says that sometimes before games, if he's on TV, you can see that he has tears in his eyes, which he attributes to the gratefulness he feels for all the things in his life.

"My time meditating up in the stands is about visualization and play calling, but the last three minutes is about getting myself in a good space. It's about not feeling like the game owes me anything, and how I'm just fortunate to be here," he said with the calm and poise of someone who'd just meditated.

Another reminder to be grateful

One can never lose sight of the fact that elite sport is hard. I found this tweet from Seattle Mariners player development coach Andy McKay to be particularly refreshing:

> *Professional baseball is hard. Travel, fatigue, failure, releases, trades, demotions, and injuries are not optional. Finding a reason to be grateful every day is a must. Without it, you become susceptible to bitterness, which doesn't help you play well. Gratitude is an advantage.*

That's it. That's the tweet.

Quiet time

In a world where we're constantly connected, it's difficult to find time to be in silence. And yet, studies suggest that quiet time is remarkably effective for those who engage in high-performance knowledge work.

Summarizing the burgeoning research into the topic, *Harvard Business Review* wrote that "silence restores the nervous system, helps sustain energy, and conditions our minds to be more adaptive and responsive to complex environments."

Sure, you're busy, but can you carve out four minutes in your day to sit in silence? I think so.

Space to think

If you're looking for Crusaders Rugby head coach Scott Robertson, you'll probably find him at Sumner Beach, just outside of Christchurch. Robertson, who boasts an 86% win record and four Super Rugby titles through his first four seasons in charge, is an avid surfer and uses his time out on the water to do his deep thinking.

"I do a lot of stand-up paddleboarding. It's an awesome way to think. It becomes quite subconscious because your body just goes with the flow of the water," he told me during our one-on-one interview.

Robertson says his time out on the water allows him to create a healthy mindset and clear his mind, but also wrestle with big challenges. "You're out to sea, away from everything, there's no distractions, and you're looking back on the world. It's a unique perspective you get as a surfer. I do a lot of my decision-making out there, and it's where a lot of my ideas come to me as well."

Many coaches believe time spent not strategizing and watching film is wasted time, as if total obsession is the key to success. It's not. And that line of thinking is not only damaging, it's untrue. We must begin to look at soul-enriching activities as valuable, and treat them as investments in ourselves and our future performance.

You don't need to learn how to surf, you just need to create time away to think and gain clarity.

Modern Elders

Time alone to think is an underutilized commodity for high-performance knowledge workers, but so is its opposite: mentorship.

For twenty-four years, Chip Conley ran boutique hotels. He was so good at it that, in 2013, Airbnb founder Brian Chesky called him and asked if he'd come and work for the rapidly growing tech company. Conley served as Airbnb's Head of Global Hospitality and Strategy for four years, during which he shared more than just hospitality know-how. What he lacked in tech-savviness he made for in soft skills and the calluses of years of experience. Channeled correctly, the generational gap generated a formidable power rather than teeth-grinding frustration.

The intergenerational mentoring he experienced at Airbnb became the inspiration for Conley's bestselling book, *Wisdom at Work*. In turn, the book became the bedrock for his idea to found the world's first midlife wisdom school, Modern Elder Academy.

Stealing Conley's idea and applying it to elite coaching would require our wisest coaches to purposely step away from coaching the team, and commit to mentoring other coaches. This would require a dramatic new system where we don't hire the 65-year-old retread coach for his twentieth new job, instead elevating him to the role of Modern Elder. "It's a new kind of elder emerging in the workplace, not the elder of the past treated with reverence, but valued for their relevance," Conley explained in an interview with *Fast Company*.

An elder with relevance

Before each game, Manchester City head coach Pep Guardiola has a pregame ritual. Directly before taking to the field, he hugs his long-time friend Manel Estiarte.

Estiarte is one of the greatest water polo players in history. The Spaniard played for his national team for twenty-three years, including twenty as captain, and led his country to a gold medal at the 1996 Atlanta Olympics.

Nowadays, Estiarte is a full-time companion for Guardiola. Explaining his role as director of first-team support, Estiarte outlines that his primary purpose is to help the head coach manage The

Weight. "My job is to help Pep, because on a day-to-day basis he is alone. It's the burden he has to carry, and I try to help him in any way I can."

While appreciative of the friendship, Guardiola also gets the benefit of being able to plug into Estiarte's finely-tuned awareness of team dynamics. "He's one of the best athletes in history, so he can read the feeling in the locker room and sense the reaction of the players and the staff," said Guardiola in a glowing assessment of the relevance Estiarte brings.

Mastermind groups

There are a multitude of support groups for CEOs, CFOs, army veterans, moms, amputees, alcoholics, rap music fans, python developers, startup founders, cosplay enthusiasts, and burrito connoisseurs. These groups connect in a variety of ways to discuss their passions, and coordinate ways they can improve their craft.

However, when it comes to head coaches in elite sport, there is a vast sea of nothingness. This gap means a majority of coaches are left without a robust network of brethren who can lend a sympathetic ear, or deliver some hard truths.

Currently, there are very few places for head coaches to go to talk about The Tough Stuff. I know because I started a coaching group of my own. I began by hand-picking some head coaches who'd be open to sharing and learning, and scheduled reoccurring calls for us. To provide them with psychological safety, I gave each coach exclusivity within their league, meaning they could speak openly without fear of their words being shared with rivals.

The first meeting was three of us, but it didn't take long to realize that some of our friends could use the sounding board as well. The next meeting had five people, then six. The group is now nine strong, from six sports, across two continents and three time zones.

When I initially started floating the idea, I was told that it would never work because 'head coaches are too busy to want to network during the season', but that has proven to be a false assumption. We've added so much value that despite their packed schedules, our members move other commitments to be on our calls. I've had some of the greatest coaches on the face of the planet call me to apologize because they have practice and have to miss one of our calls. What this says to me is that the opportunities afforded to them in the past have been insufficient, and when presented with a valuable, useful ninety minutes of peer-to-peer support, coaches will move heaven and earth to be there.

In my mind, the real benefit of our coaching club is that—just like alcoholics and python developers and cosplay enthusiasts—when we get together and share The Tough Stuff, we all realize we're not as crazy as we'd previously thought. Whatever the sport, whatever the level, head coaches all have the same problems, vulnerabilities, fears, and irrationalities.

It's about time that head coaches started banding together and supporting each other. As a matter of urgency, I suggest you incisively go about designing a robust support network made up of current and former head coaches. Only other CEOs can truly comprehend The Weight and The Tough Stuff that go along with the title, and head coaches are no different.

We are better together.

Key Takeaways

1. You're a high-performance knowledge worker. The cognitive demands of head coaching require preparation and rewiring of your base brain state.

2. Get. Some. Sleep.

3. Your nutrition and exercise regimen should be as stringently tailored as your players' programs.

4. It's okay to think of yourself as an asset and prioritize your performance. For your team to perform at its optimum, you need to perform at your optimum.

5. Mentoring and companionship are underrated. There's a reason there are so many CEO groups; each and every member understands the plight and can offer support.

*"Words are, of course, the most
powerful drug used by mankind."*

Rudyard Kipling

Every word counts

6

Keep your eye on the ball

It was meant to be a cute video that brought a smile to your face, but it doubled as a crucial coaching lesson. A father is teaching his young son how to swing a baseball bat by hitting balls off a tee. The boy, who can't be much older than two, hits the first ball and lets out an enthusiastic squeal. As the father tees up another ball, he says, "Remember: keep your eye on the ball." Immediately, the kid seems confused. "Eye on the ball, eye on the ball," the father reiterates as his son processes the new instruction.

Then, the child does exactly what you'd expect. With the ball perched motionless on the tee, he bends forward and places his eye socket on top of the ball.

He'd taken it literally.

The video brings to light the power of communication and reiterates the importance of the words we choose to use when coaching athletes.

Now that I've planted the seed, I'm sure you can think of a handful of sayings from your sport that don't make much sense. As coaches, we must be aware of these default sayings and recognize that they have the potential to be as disruptive to progress as any other intervention we attempt.

Illusions of mastery

As humans, we like to think we're good communicators, but I'm not so sure that's true.

We struggle to find words that appropriately communicate our feelings. We are uncomfortable with silence so we say too much and confuse the original message. We fabricate conversations in our heads. We shy away from difficult dialogue. We're bad at constructive disagreement. We interpret conversations differently than they were intended, and then change the meaning of those conversations over time. We've taught ourselves that a good presentation is when the speaker doesn't pause from their script for sixty minutes. And so the list goes on.

Many of our struggles can be traced back to two issues: the words we allocate to things ("Keep your eye on the ball"), and how we think about communication. In my mind, both of these require a rethink.

Rethinking communication

First, let's fix the framework by changing how we think about communication. Traditionally, there are considered to be five types of communication: verbal, non-verbal, visual, written, and listening. This framework is overly simplistic and overlooks the two types of communication that occur most often—self-talk and behavior.

Both are generally partitioned off as psychological disciplines, which makes sense from an academic research perspective but greatly hinders us in practice. How you speak to yourself and the actions you take on a day-by-day basis combine to produce the physical embodiment of how you perceive the world and your role in it. If there's one thing you take away from this book, I hope it's that your words and actions are the greatest communication tools available to any head coach looking to raise their game.

It's my strong belief that there are seven types of communication that we should be looking to develop:

1. **Verbal** (spoken word)
2. **Self-talk** (inner voice)
3. **Non-verbal** (expression and body language)

4. **Behavior** (actions)
5. **Visual** (images, videos, memes)
6. **Written** (letters, texts, emails)
7. **Listening** (hearing and interpreting)

By including self-talk and behavior as their own forms of communication (rather than traits that only a psychologist can fix), we can begin to work on upgrading our level of mastery with them. This, without doubt, will filter into our coaching.

For the rest of this chapter, we'll explore the seven types of communication, and continue to challenge common words and phrases used in coach speak. The good news is, as you'll see, it only takes small adjustments to make a big difference.

Language shapes our reality

The Thaayorre are an indigenous people from the northernmost tip of mainland Australia, and they have an interesting quirk to their native language, known as Kuuk Thaayorre.

In her TED talk, cognitive scientist Lera Boroditsky explains that the Thaayorre don't use words like left or right, instead using cardinal direction; north, south, east, and west. "You would say something like 'there's an ant on my south-west leg.'" Direction also forms the basis for their customary greeting, as well as how they think about and organize time.

Previously, the scientific community believed that humans were poor at staying oriented to direction, but as Boroditsky points out, "if your language and your culture train you to do it, you can do it."

There are also more granular ways that language shapes how humans perceive the world, like how we count or divide up the color spectrum. "Some languages have lots of words for colors, and some only have a few, like light and dark," Boroditsky outlined, before pointing out how English speakers and Russian speakers account for different shades of blue.

Boroditsky's work is particularly pertinent given how much of our success as head coaches is based on our ability to use language and culture to shape the realities of our players. For all of the things we do as coaches, being an elite communicator is perhaps the most important. Our players' ability to solve problems together on-field is based on the language we give them. Our ability to have our values come to life through experiences is based on the language we choose for them. And who they become as people away from the facility is based on the language we reinforce for them inside their heads.

If language shapes how humans perceive the world, it behooves you as a coach to concern yourself with the language profile of each of your players. As nations become more global, understanding native languages and how different cultures perceive the world has become increasingly important.

Your hockey team might import a Swedish player (who brings her own language profile from Sweden) but let's say her parents were Bosnian refugees. Now you're dealing with someone who potentially thinks and dreams in Bosnian, speaks in Swedish, and plays hockey in English. Or, if you happened to coach someone from the Thaayorre, telling them that your team wants to play 'north-south' would cause all sorts of confusion.

East vs. West

To support Boroditsky's findings, there is a burgeoning thread of neuroscience dedicated to understanding how languages and cultures shape the way different people learn. In one study, Chinese-born and American-born participants were shown a wide array of images, with the researchers tracking and comparing their eye movements.

While the American participants focused sooner and longer on the focal objects, the Chinese participants had a more balanced focus on both the focal object and the background. In other words, the Americans were searching for specifics, the Chinese were searching for context. The researchers attributed the results to cultural nuances, namely that Eastern cultures promote social cohesion and interdependence, whereas Western cultures seek autonomy and independence.

As coaches, we tend to assume everyone takes away the same information from visual cues (e.g., game films, a play diagram, or a game plan document), however this may not be true. Depending on where your player, or your staff member, was raised, they may perceive that visual cue differently, and memorize it with varying degrees of effectiveness.

This presents an exciting opportunity for us to rethink how our communication could be targeted to the recipient so it not only resonates better, but can also be recalled more easily. And isn't that precisely what we're there to do?

People have changed; coaching has changed

It wasn't too long ago that players did what the coach said. No questions asked. Those command-and-control days are over. It's not that a coach's expertise or authority have diminished, it's that players will no longer blindly follow you just because of your title. They want to understand; they want to participate; they want to co-create; they want to connect.

Language as a connector (Part I)

About twenty miles outside of Birmingham, England is Wolverhampton, a city known for being the birthplace of one of the members of One Direction, its art galleries, and its soccer club. Wolverhampton Wanderers, or 'Wolves' as they're commonly known, were a powerhouse team in the 1950s, with their attractive style of playing drawing many fans, including a young George Best.

Since those halcyon days, the club has gone bankrupt twice and drifted up and down the English footballing pyramid. After being purchased by a Chinese conglomerate in 2016, Wolves have experienced a rapid on-field renaissance, culminating in the team qualifying for the Europa League quarter-finals in 2019-20.

While money and resources always help, language has played a key role in Wolves' audacious leap into prominence. Currently, Wolverhampton has eleven Portuguese players in their first team squad, as well as two Brazilians (who speak Portuguese), three Spaniards, and two other starting players who used to play for major Portuguese clubs. Guiding them all is Portuguese head coach Nuno Espirito Santo and his band of (mostly) Portuguese support staff. Many of the players speak fluent English, but the ability to avoid confusion by communicating in Portuguese is undoubtedly a source of competitive advantage.

The recruiting tactic was initially laughed at, but has proven a stroke of genius for the club. The English Premier League is the fastest and most physical league in European soccer and is notoriously difficult to transition into. Many talented players have struggled to adapt. Yet, one after the other, Wolves keep hiring Portuguese players and having them slide seamlessly into their cohesive team.

Language as a connector (Part II)

American soccer head coach Jesse Marsch, who we met in a previous chapter, sprung to notoriety when one of his team talks was released on social media.

With Red Bull Salzburg trailing 1-3 to Liverpool at half-time of their Champions League encounter, Marsch decided to roll up his sleeves and deliver a big rousing speech—in German.

"Whenever I see videos of myself trying to speak German it's always incredibly embarrassing," he told *The Independent* in an interview about the viral video. Marsch's passionate message was held together by English filler (and English swear words), but that wasn't the point. "There's two things that come along with me speaking German. There's an adaptation to the culture, which includes understanding how the people work and how they think and how they talk, and there's also showing my vulnerability, the imperfection of who I am," he explained thoughtfully.

While his team talk did inspire a comeback (Salzburg drew level 15 minutes into the second half), Marsch's communication tactic was about creating a mindset of longevity that extended well beyond that game against Liverpool.

"We have a lot of young players in our team and they have to know that making mistakes is okay," the coach said. "If you know German fluently and you listen to me speaking German, literally every sentence I make mistakes. So it's then a chance for me to show improvement, show vulnerability, and work through it personally."

Your big rousing speech

Some movie buffs consider Al Pacino's 'inches' speech from the movie *Any Given Sunday* to be the best sports movie soliloquy of all-time. I used to be able to recite it word-for-word.

The subtext to the speech, though, is that Pacino's character, Tony D'Amato, gives the address to soothe his own woes. While he eventually links it back to football, a majority of the monologue focuses on the head coach's reflections on his own life, loss, age, and alcoholism.

The entirety of *Any Given Sunday* is a caricature of modern professional football, but Pacino's speech stands out as one of the most authentic parts of the movie. Why? Because many coaches do indeed give team talks for themselves more than their team. Perhaps worse is that these big rousing speeches have become the yardstick for what many people consider good coaching.

It doesn't need to be that way.

"We've taken the attitude that if you have to do a team talk on gameday then it's too late," said former All Blacks head coach Steve Hansen, who won 86% of his matches in charge of New Zealand's iconic rugby team.

Rest assured, though, Hansen's removal of team talks was not a move borne of arrogance. Rather, he believed that if his coaching staff used their preparation time during the week to provide clarity of expectations, a traditional pregame motivational speech was superfluous. In an interview with the *New Zealand Herald*, Hansen explained, "We agree early in the week on what messages are going to be important and quietly go about delivering them. You get down to the business end of the week and you start handing complete control over to the people who are going to play the game."

Last-minute motivation, he surmised, wasn't required because you simply don't get to be an All Black if you're not self-motivated.

As for gameday, Hansen believed his duty was to make sure his players were clear on their role and confident in their mind. "You might give a quiet word to an individual but you certainly don't have to do a rah-rah speech," he added.

Philadelphia 76ers head coach Doc Rivers, who coached the Boston Celtics to the 2008 NBA title, concurs. "Rah-rah speeches are overrated." Rivers said flatly, "There's no secret speech. That's for the movies. The real thing is you've got to have the players prepared."

Are you someone who gives a big rousing speech because you think that's what good coaching is? Could it be something you use sporadically, rather than every game? And have you taken the time to consider whether you're giving a big rousing speech for your team, or is it for you?

You shouldn't have to have an 86% win ratio or be an NBA champion to be able to reconsider whether the traditions of communicating as a coach are outdated, and whether they're helping or hindering your team.

More is not always better

There aren't many people who embody the term 'pure coach' better than former Toronto Raptors and Phoenix Suns head coach Jay Triano. Now an assistant coach with the Charlotte Hornets, Triano visits Toronto regularly as the away team, and on one such visit he invited me to the team hotel to chat.

As happens when coaches get together, the conversation went straight into coaching theory, and we began talking about how many messages a player retains during a game. I asked Triano to think back to his playing career, which included captaining Canada at two Olympics, and pressed him on how many pieces of information he recalls being able to remember after half-time breaks. "Maybe three, and the third one was probably a stretch," he said. I agreed, adding that I found once I was back in the heat of the action, the first two instructions remained crystal clear, but the third was always foggy.

Just like the pregame talk, in-game messaging tends to default to what feels optimal for the coach, with every second of a timeout loaded with information so that the coach can comfort themselves by saying, 'Well, I told them that would happen!'

This info-packing doesn't only occur in-game either. In a recent study of one-on-one game tape reviews in the AFL, it was found that a coach offered up around sixteen pieces of feedback every ten minutes. Some of the meetings studied touched thirty minutes, meaning around forty-eight messages were delivered to the player. A week later, the players were asked to recount specifics from the one-on-one feedback sessions to measure how much they'd taken in and retained over time.

The players were able to recall 50% of broad topics that a coach had talked to them about, and only 6% of the more granular feedback. If this is anything to go by, your players retain half of your general instructions, and can recall the actual sentence you used just one-tenth of the time. You better choose wisely which messages you want them to retain.

In-the-moment feedback

Study after study suggests that people at all levels want timely and honest feedback about their work. As coaches, we often do well with the honest part, but fail to address the timely.

Former Atlanta Falcons head coach Dan Quinn believes the best coaches he's been around are those who are able to deliver feedback to players immediately. "The best of the best are able to talk about the smallest of details—a change in body position or a change in technique, and they deliver that to the player in-the-moment. If you wait too long, it's easy to disassociate from the play and for your feedback to feel like discipline. It doesn't need to be a long lecture, but I believe it does need to be instant," Quinn told me.

Obviously, there are logistical challenges to always delivering immediate feedback, and American Football is a sport with built-in coaching breaks. However, I agree wholeheartedly with Coach Quinn on this point. The prevalence of video has made coaches lazy and trained them to wait to analyze the tape.

The essence of coaching is being able to describe to someone what happened in real-time, to spot a trend or recognize a poor technique. "To me, it should be like a tweet—short and concise. That's the best in-the-moment coaching," Quinn added decisively.

Praise

Through the early stages of the COVID-19 lockdown, I put on a webinar series with sport science pioneer Fergus Connolly. In one session focused on feedback, Fergus and I couldn't agree on how we personally like to be praised.

I offered that I enjoyed hearing comments such as 'I'm proud of you' and 'I appreciate you', while Fergus found those phrases to be patronizing. Conversely, Fergus appreciated praise like 'I'm happy for you,' which to me sounds like a sassy brush-off.

The learning is that there is no one-size-fits-all solution, even when it comes to something like positive reinforcement. You should ask your players and staff how they like to be praised and whether there are any common phrases that they find cringeworthy.

(It's also safe to assume that "good job" is both lousy praise, and downright lazy).

"You don't have to be an asshole"

Delivering bad news to people is one of the most agonizing duties of a head coach. To make matters worse, recent studies have shown that messengers of bad news are unfairly deemed malicious and incompetent, with the ill-will escalating even further if the recipient is not a fan of the messenger to begin with.

For many coaches, delivering bad news is a daily occurrence when picking teams or managing rosters. We can deflect the emotional toll by framing the industry as 'a business', but that doesn't necessarily make it any easier.

For too long, the prevalent advice has been to take emotion out of it when delivering bad news. It's horrible advice. You can't spend months and years together, referring to yourselves as a 'family' and 'brothers', and then turn around and say emotion shouldn't be present during difficult conversations.

Even in the cut-throat world of the NFL, Dan Quinn believes in a more human approach to delivering bad news. "You have to say the hard things to people, but I don't necessarily think you have to say them in a hard way. You don't have to be an asshole," he asserted.

One way to navigate the emotional landscape of bad news is to acknowledge that it's tough for you to be the messenger, and then focus on being of service to the receiver. If you care deeply about them, you'll go above and beyond to help them continue to progress in their life journey or athletic endeavor.

Oh, how it stings

In a post-match debrief, Usman Khawaja nervously looked around, shifting his eyes from the ground to his teammates, and eventually over to the head coach, who he was sitting directly beside. "I think the boys are intimidated by you, Alf; there's a bit of walking on eggshells going on," Khawaja offered passively.

Justin Langer (whose nickname is Alfie after famous rugby league player Allan 'Alfie' Langer) took over coaching the Australian men's cricket team after a cheating scandal that rocked the country's national sport. Langer's job was challenging yet straightforward: rebuild the culture and restore faith in a team that has long dictated the mood of 25-million Australians.

Langer is an advocate of honest and transparent feedback, yet the smirk-turned-grimace on his face suggested he was stinging from the criticism leveled at him by one of his senior players.

"So, you're specifically talking about me?" Langer barked back at Khawaja, who calmly responded, "I feel like the boys are afraid to say it." As Langer looks away and grabs a sip of his drink, Khawaja continues to articulate his feedback in front of the entire team. Watching the exchange, captured in the documentary series *The Test*, I could empathize with Langer. While he knows the discourse is productive and necessary, his face was that of a parent who'd been told by their child that their love and support is too overbearing.

The popular narrative is that candid criticism is great and we should welcome it (which we should), but it doesn't change the fact that it can sting when we receive it. We are human, after all.

The power of the inner voice

In 2016, my friend Travis McKenzie and I launched a first-person storytelling site called *InnerVoice*. Our concept was simple: we wanted to document what was going through the minds of endurance athletes, those who are pushing the limits of human performance.

Over the course of three years, InnerVoice amassed millions of reads as we shed new light on the mindsets and motivations of the world's best triathletes, cyclists, runners, and swimmers.

We interviewed dozens of elite-level guests, headlined by Ironman champions Tim Don, Ben Kanute, Liz Blatchford, and Helle Frederiksen; Olympians Laura Brown, Kikkan Randall, Colleen Quigley, and Kara Goucher; Boston Marathon winner Des Linden; Barkley Marathons finisher John Kelly; World Tour cyclists Michael Woods, Ted King, Brent Bookwalter, and Coryn Rivera; adventurer Colin O'Brady; mountain bike world champion Kate Courtney; and channel swimmer Jessi Harewicz. On the odd occasion, we even ventured outside of professional athletics and interviewed performers who use the endurance disciplines as a hobby and stress reliever, like actor Patrick Dempsey, celebrity chef Jeff Mahin, and IWC CEO Christoph Grainger-Herr.

What was most fascinating for me was how easy it was for endurance athletes to describe their inner voice. Whether they were a world champion or weekend warrior, they could recall intimate details of conversations they'd had with themselves throughout training and competition.

Almost all endurance athletes train their inner voice and have preferred mantras or sayings, but they also have backups, and backups to the backups. They become experts in self-negotiation, sometimes to urge themselves to keep going, sometimes to do whatever they can not to shit themselves during a televised race (seriously, this came up).

But that was the point of the site: when the human body is at its absolute limit and on the brink of shutting down, what is the conversation going on in your head?

What many of the athletes were able to describe was having a state of emotional agility. As their bodies were at the brink, they would have such visceral interactions with their emotions that they often refused to label them as good or bad, preferring instead to recognize each emotion for its power. It is often seen as a 'negative' emotion, but more than one athlete told me about using anger to get over a bout of mid-race exhaustion.

For me, the *InnerVoice* project proved to be an education on the power of the human mind, and changed everything I believed to be true about how we communicate with ourselves. It also changed how I communicate with myself.

In fact, I believe the greatest leap in my communication skill came from upgrading the vocabulary of my inner voice. Inspired by the great endurance athletes I'd met, I began showing myself some self-love, positive reinforcement, and calming words. Now, I'm able to navigate the inevitable ups and downs of the day with more consistency. In turn, this has helped my ability to present complex ideas to my players via presentations, remain calm in stressful environments, and improve my general demeanor.

Locker room language

At the Atlanta Falcons, Dan Quinn created a culture that was meticulous with its communication. "Head coaches need to understand that the messaging not only has to come from you, but also from the staff or the people associated with the team," he explained.

Quinn believes in including his backroom team and medical staff in team meetings, even if they don't have direct responsibility for the topics covered. When I pressed him on why, Quinn said he didn't have the time for one-on-one conversations with every player, every day. But the staff did. They could be the messengers.

So how did he know when a message had been communicated effectively? "I knew we'd done a good job with a topic when I told the assistant coaches, and then later on in the day I heard the players talking about the same topic, using the same language, in the locker room," he said.

The impact of being in the room

High-performance guru Darren Burgess attributes some of his success in elite sport to simply being in the room with the head coach. In a career that's included stops at Arsenal, Liverpool, Australia's men's national soccer team, Port Adelaide Power, and the Melbourne Demons, Burgess has been able to work with some of the most influential coaches in world sport.

"I've been really lucky that for the last twenty years, I've been in every single coaches meeting, every single tactics meeting," he told me in a phone conversation. Burgess continued: "I've been able to observe and hear the coaches' struggles and the work that goes into preparing a session, or preparing for a game."

Breakdowns in communication are often the result of excluding key people from being in the room. If your performance, medical, and operations staff aren't in the meetings, they are going to pass on messages that they think are right, in their own context, rather than reiterating your key messages.

Reading the room

Not long after he left his head coaching role at Tottenham Hotspur, Mauricio Pochettino gave an interview on *The High Performance Podcast*. When asked what he does when he gets negative vibes from the team, the Argentinian gave a decisive answer:

> *"You have to find out why. When you arrive in the morning, you plan to do a particular training session. But when you feel the energy of the group, you might change the plan. We might have some meetings, but when I shake hands with the players, I might decide to change the meetings.*
>
> *It's so important to have a plan, but you must also be aware of what the players need or what the team needs in that moment. Football is like this, it's about making decisions in the moment, based on how you feel."*

You won't often read about feeling during a chapter about communication, but being able to read energy might be one of the defining characteristics of the coaches we look to as standouts. Their clairvoyant awareness mixed with their decisiveness to change the plan to suit the needs of the players may indeed be what we ascribe as good coaching—although we often talk about it through a vehicle of wins or trophies or over-performance.

Coach mode

Dan Quinn says the art of coaching is the ability to communicate, and sometimes that communication is simply listening. After the Black Lives Matter protests on the streets of Atlanta, Quinn had a meeting with a group of his Falcons players.

"I was ready to go into Coach Mode: How can I fix it? But I was glad that I didn't because the players weren't ready, they were just mad and they wanted a chance to talk and be pissed off about what had happened," he told me candidly. "If I'd gone into Coach Mode, I would've totally missed the moment and the ability to hear about their experiences."

It's an important lesson for all leaders, who so easily want to go into Coach Mode and fix problems. If you don't create the space to listen, you'll miss out on a lot of different perspectives that can help you make better decisions. Coach Mode isn't always the best mode.

The leader is the biggest barrier

I've found that it's not particularly interesting to ask a head coach what their cultural non-negotiables are. Rather, it's fascinating to ask how many of their non-negotiables they adhere to themselves.

According to former Sydney Swans head coach Paul Roos, this is where many head coaches fall down. "Leaders often struggle implementing team behaviors because their own behaviors are so poor," he said on my podcast.

Under Roos, the Swans became known as the culture club of the AFL, renowned for their disciplined play and stifling defense. Their strong sense of historical identity and ruthless commitment to their culture allowed Sydney to win the 2005 championship, and set in motion a league-wide cultural revolution that is still in effect today.

Rival clubs wanted a piece of what the Swans had built, which at its core was an agreed-upon set of behaviors and standards that drove everything they did. Roos says it's important to recognize this wasn't your stereotypical 'do as I say, not as I do' type of environment, and that his behaviors were under scrutiny and open to candid discussion just like the players.

"If you have a leader who can't adhere to the behaviors, it's very difficult for that leader to then set standards. The coach is the role model that everyone looks to," Roos added, noting that if he had his way, leaders would be renamed 'role models' to better reflect their duties and responsibilities.

In copying Roos' team design, many organizations have failed because they imitated surface-level activities without understanding the core principles. "It's exhausting to be a leader. To be a great leader, you have to communicate," Roos added emphatically. "The missing piece, often, is you've got to create the framework around what communication is. It's great to have candid communication, but if you don't know what your behaviors are, it's very hard to know what you're communicating about."

It's a worthwhile exercise to ask whether or not your team communication is rooted in agreed-upon behaviors, or if you're just stabbing in the dark.

Being approachable

When he was high-performance director at Arsenal, Darren Burgess worked closely with head coach Arsène Wenger to arrest the team's growing injury concerns. Wenger is widely acknowledged as the coach who heightened the level of science in the Premier League, but his long history of winning and iconic status in the game did have drawbacks when it came to communication.

"In one of my first weeks at Arsenal, there was a lineup outside of Arsène's office. They were waiting for him to come out before they spoke to him," Burgess reminisced. "I opened the door and he was sitting there planning the training session. I asked my question, and just walked back out again. The other staff members were too intimidated to disturb him, because he had this aura about him."

Burgess says the staff needed not be intimidated by Wenger. "I can't think of a time he didn't take my recommendation. If I went up to Arsène and told him that Mesut Özil didn't sleep well and I wanted to pull him from a training drill, Arsène would look at me and say, 'Okay!'"

The culprit here isn't Wenger and it isn't the staff, it's power dynamics. Head coaches need to be aware that tending to the power dynamics (perceived or real) within your organization is key to breaking down the barriers of communication. Humans come pre-conditioned with all sorts of anxieties and fears about authority figures, so regardless of how approachable you think you are, you're always fighting against their personal histories.

They need to see me doing it

George Washington Colonials men's basketball coach Jamion Christian says that his team's meditation practice is one of the first things they install every season. His team brings in an expert whose job it is to teach meditation and mindfulness to two or three of the players, who are in-turn responsible for teaching it to the group. The players meditate as a team every day, and spend five minutes meditating right before they hit the floor for tipoff.

"I think there's a different vibe when it's player-led, but it's also important that I practice. They need to see me doing it so they know I think it's valuable," he stated emphatically.

A modern head coach if ever I've met one, Christian understands that modeling the behavior he's encouraging from his players is the most effective way to communicate its importance. Otherwise, it's just lip-service.

For all his personal enthusiasm about meditation and its impact on individual and team performance, he's still disrupting the apple cart of how things are done in basketball. Teams don't meditate before games. Certainly not right before tipoff. With that in mind, I quizzed Christian about how his players viewed the change in preparation. "Now, when they see me meditating, no-one even blinks," he responded, "Or, if a player is meditating on the bench, the rest of the players know exactly what's going on. It's great!"

Just give me a sign

In 1963, the prank show *Candid Camera* showed how easy it is to shape people with language. Standing on the side of the highway at the Pennsylvania-Delaware border, an ordinary man wearing an 'official looking hat' held a sign reading "Delaware Closed Today."

The stunt stopped traffic, with many turning around to return to Pennsylvania. According to news reports, one woman even asked if New Jersey was open and said she'd be happy to go there instead.

One conclusion from the miniature social experiment is that people are gullible. A more thoughtful takeaway, though, is that words hold enormous power to shape people's behavior.

Working with your players

In a television interview, legendary UCLA basketball coach John Wooden told a story about what he learned from observing a press conference when Wilt Chamberlain arrived at the Los Angeles Lakers in 1968.

Responding to a question from a journalist about the impression he was difficult for coaches to handle, Chamberlain said, "No one handles me. I am not a thing, I am a person. You handle things, you work with people."

For Coach Wooden, a lightbulb went off. He'd just published his book *Practical Modern Basketball,* and in it he had a section titled 'Handling Your Players'. Wooden raced home and marked out all of the places he'd used the phrase 'handling your players' and asked the publisher to replace them with 'working with your players'.

What your players hear

Michael Maguire has coached championship teams in both of the world's premier rugby league competitions. In England in 2010, he coached the country's powerhouse team, Wigan Warriors, to their first Super League title in over a decade. Shortly after, he returned home to Australia and led the Russell Crowe-owned South Sydney Rabbitohs to their first title since 1971.

In Tom Young's excellent book, *The Making of a Leader,* Maguire speaks openly of his understanding that when talking to the media, he's never just talking to the media. "What I am saying on camera, one of my players can take the wrong way," he explained, adding, "A player might think 'Well, hang on, he is talking about something he just spoke to me about,' and you might not have knowledge that the player has seen it that way."

This type of communication breakdown isn't confined to coaching. You may have experienced it in your own life. Your partner may make a generic comment about cleaning that you interpret as being aimed at you because you haven't vacuumed the floors yet. When receiving the message, you add your own insecurities and venom to the message, even though it may not be intended that way. In the soundbite world of sports media, the ability for these messages to get hijacked is greater than ever before, and something that is worth deliberately addressing with your team on a consistent basis. It's best, I believe, to set a standard that for better or worse, you'll never talk to your team through the media. We're all adults; we have our conversations directly, even if they're unpleasant.

Just listen

When I interviewed Iowa Hawkeyes football head coach Kirk Ferentz on my podcast, I was keen to ask him what he learned from working with Bill Belichick. Many onlookers associate Belichick with his tactical innovations or gruff media persona, but I don't believe you can create what he's created without an outstanding level of emotional intelligence.

Ferentz confirmed my assumption in a surprising way:

> *"The thing that amazed me over my three years of working with Coach Belichick, and it really hit me right in the face when I got to Cleveland, is that he's an unbelievable listener. That's not always a trait that you associate with people that are head coaches.*
>
> *He is really curious, he'll ask great questions and then is actively listening and absorbing. You might say something and think it's the end of it, but six weeks later, he'll reference it in a conversation."*

Coaches fantasize about being referred to as a great communicator. But I think that a more sought-after label should be 'unbelievable listener'. What are you doing to actively listen and absorb from the people in your team?

Every word counts

The art of coaching lies in the ability to communicate effectively. Previously, head coaches prided themselves on their ability to explain a training drill or give a big rousing speech. As we've just explored, it's a lot more intricate than that, and the words you don't say can be the ones that communicate the most.

I'll leave you with a mantra that sport psychologist Brian

Levenson passed on to me that I've found to be useful. Brian suggested that I use the phrase "talk to yourself more than you listen to yourself" as a reminder when things get messy or stressful. It means to talk yourself into, or out of, situations based on your rational voice rather than listening to your raw emotions.

It's gems like this that reinforce the need for us to include self-talk as a form of communication.

Key Takeaways

1. There are seven types of communication (verbal, non-verbal, self-talk, written, visual, behavior, and listening). All are skills we should work to upgrade.

2. Language and culture shape how we perceive the world, and should shape how we coach our players.

3. Upgrading the vocabulary of your inner voice might be the greatest leap you can make as a coach.

4. If you want to instill habits on your players, you as the head coach must exhibit them, too. Behavior is a form of communication.

5. Including cultural influencers in conversations helps protect from gossip and dissent. Your biggest allies to instilling a culture might be the boot studder or physio. Include them in conversations.

"Basketball is a great mystery.
You can do everything right. You can have the perfect mix
of talent and system. But if your players don't have a sense
of oneness as a group, your efforts won't pay off.
The bond that unites a team can be so fragile, so elusive."

Phil Jackson

Tactics don't really matter

7

Building cohesive teams

The magic of sport is that each game presents us with a raft of constraints, and there are a myriad of ways in which we can choose to work within them. You can win games with a miserly defense or an expansive offense, breathtaking foot speed or towering physical dominance, supreme technical ability or brute force.

In my years of researching why teams win, one thing has become abundantly clear. Teams don't win because of tactical superiority; they win because their players can execute *whichever tactics they choose* at a faster pace—with consistency and greater intensity—for longer. I've seen teams dominate leagues with highly intricate tactical game plans, and I've seen teams dominate leagues with tactical game plans no more advanced than you'd see in Under-7s. The point is, it's not the tactics unto themselves.

This isn't just an opinion, either. GainLine Analytics are heading up the study of team cohesion, and one of their key markers of team success is time spent playing together. By accumulating continuity in-season and across seasons, players become more familiar with each other and the linkages between them become stronger. It is these strong bonds that allow teams to implement tactics at a faster pace, with consistency and greater intensity, for longer.

GainLine's work has turned up other interesting tidbits that have the potential to take coaching to a new level, such as a study on rugby which suggested teams who lost were more likely to win the next week if they didn't change their starting lineup.

This might seem counter-intuitive, since we traditionally equate losing to tactical inferiority—often swapping out players to get a better result next time. But if you equate winning to time spent playing together, you're more likely to give your players the opportunity to strengthen that cohesion.

I believe it's time we put the tactics books down and look at what high-cohesion, high-connection activities can help us deliver the results we're after. By strengthening the linkages between our players, we put in place a framework that allows us to implement a whole range of new tactical options. In short, by building a cohesive team, you'll come away looking like a tactical genius anyway.

This chapter looks at the head coaches who've already taken giant steps towards creating connected and cohesive environments.

Seamwork

I'm yet to meet a head coach who got into coaching to oversee a vast hierarchy and become an expert in delegation and organizational dynamics. Yet, it is today's reality that the head coaching role has become something akin to a corporate CEO.

Like a CEO, the most impactful thing a modern coach can spend their time on is the seams between the individuals, teams, and departments. This 'seamwork' is about breaking down silos, opening up communication networks, and sealing the gaps that, under duress, have the potential to derail any successful team.

Dysfunctional staffs

Often, where seamwork is needed most is between the staff. As coaches, we focus endlessly on cultivating the culture amongst our players, exonerating the staff from responsibility for their role in the healthy functioning of the culture. It's easy to point the finger at disruptive players, but I've also heard countless stories of coaching staffs that can barely get through a constructive conversation together.

Iowa Hawkeyes football head coach Kirk Ferentz spoke of this precise dynamic when I interviewed him on my podcast, saying, "In college football, we have 100 players on our roster. It's really hard to expect them to act as a team and work as a team, if the staff that they're working with isn't doing that."

Under Ferentz, Iowa has become a talent goldmine, regularly recruiting underappreciated players from high school and then developing them into high NFL draft picks. The Hawkeyes have also seen team success under Ferentz, twice capturing the Big10 championship and winning nine Bowl games—the most under any coach in school history.

"Players aren't stupid, they know what's going on. They can sense phoniness; they can sense dysfunction," he added with an air of authority. "If your staff are on the same page, it gives you a chance to have your team be together. It's as simple as that. Team success starts with the people involved as coaches. We're all different, but when we're together, we have to be together."

Are you spending time building connection between your staff, or are you expecting it to just click?

Multipliers

Liz Wiseman is the bestselling author of *Multipliers*, and has conducted a significant amount of research into leadership and collective intelligence. In her book, Wiseman suggests that leaders who are Multipliers are effective in two ways: by extracting intelligence out of their people, and then extending that intelligence to achieve greater results. Diminishers, on the other hand, consider themselves to be of supreme intelligence and that other people will never figure things out without them.

While Wiseman's work is focused specifically on the leader, Ryerson Rams women's basketball head coach Carly Clarke has adapted the ideas for her culture. "In elite sport, you need talent to win. But you can look at your culture as a multiplier of that talent," she told me. "I think about it like this: where you have good talent and multiply it with great culture, you can do something special, and where you have great talent and multiply it with great culture, you really have a chance at sustained success."

Whether the leader or the culture is the Multiplier, the only way for it to work is to believe that talent and intelligence lie within each of your players, and to be obsessed with drawing it out and amplifying it. The second you default to sayings like "we have no talent" is the second you become a Diminisher.

Why isn't enough

Author Simon Sinek changed the world with his bestseller, *Start With Why*, but as the title suggests, it's only a good starting place. Understanding your internal motivation (or 'Why') in elite sport is pretty simple, but your cause loses some of its power when it's everyone else's cause as well.

In his book, *The Score Takes Care of Itself*, legendary San Francisco 49ers head coach Bill Walsh wrote the following: "Combat soldiers talk about who they will die for. It's those guys right next to them in the trench, not the fight song, the flag, or some general back at the Pentagon. 'I couldn't let my buddies down' is what they all say."

What Walsh hit on is the missing piece to Sinek's Why equation. Everyone in elite sport understands that the cause is to win, and they're all motivated by it to a certain degree. But what's missing is human connection. In my mind, the most potent combination any team in elite sport can possess is cause and connection.

Care more

Roy Rana is a legend in Canadian basketball after coaching Team Canada to a gold medal at the U19 World Cup. Rana worked his way up from high school to Canadian college basketball, and is now an assistant coach with the NBA's Sacramento Kings.

Over lunch one day in Toronto, Roy and I started talking about building robust cultures. At one point, he turned to me and asked, "If you had to boil it down to one thing, what sets apart the truly great organizations?"

After pausing to think, I said, "They care more."

When I say 'care', I don't mean it in a vacant, pretendy way. I mean that the sports teams we revere for their sustained success, they attack seamwork better than their rivals.

They go deeper than surface level and look after not just their players, but the people that their players care about—their partners, parents, and children.

They care about lapses in communication.

They care about lapses in discipline.

They unashamedly use words like 'love'.

They love each other long after they've ceased being teammates.

They care about human beings, even in a cutthroat industry where people are treated as 'assets' to be traded.

If you're looking to create long-lasting success for your organization, the recipe is rather simple: care more!

When knowledge is no longer power

When Connacht Rugby head coach Andy Friend started coaching in the early 90s, knowledge was power. In the pre-internet era, coaches could hoard knowledge and use it to create competitive advantage. Now, knowledge has been commoditized, so where is the point of difference for a coach?

I asked that question to Friend, to which he responded: "To me, the point of difference is your emotional attachment and emotional intelligence; your ability to connect and commit to various types of people and support them emotionally, rather than tactical or strategically."

For Friend, who came through as a skills coach, the role of connector-as-coach feels more natural to him. "As a head coach, your job is now about the people. My philosophy of rugby is 'know the game, coach the individual', so while I love strategy and tactics, for me it's always been about connection. The way the coaching movement has gone, it's ended up in an area that I'm much more comfortable in," he riffed.

Andy Friend is a multiplier who cares more, and it shows in his team's performances. Just before going to print, his young Connacht team traveled to Dublin and beat three-time Pro14 defending champions Leinster, not just the best team in their league, potentially the best team in all of Europe.

Get to know them (Part I)

In October 2018, the Minnesota Twins made 37-year-old Rocco Baldelli the youngest head coach in Major League Baseball. As a player, Baldelli was a star on the rise, being likened to a young Joe DiMaggio. Cruelly, injuries and a muscle disorder derailed his career before he could truly reach his peak. Within four seasons of retiring, Baldelli had made such inroads as a coach that he interviewed for five out of the six head coaching vacancies that off-season.

And when you analyze the exchange below with a reporter during his introductory press conference, it's not difficult to understand why he was in such high demand:

Reporter:

"This is your first job, everybody knows you're the youngest manager in Major League Baseball. How do you get these guys to believe in what you're telling them, with your limited experience?"

Baldelli:

"I think you talk to them. You don't come out the first day and give your semi-interesting spring training speech to the whole team and hope that's going to do the trick. That's not how it works.

The way it works is, you talk to the players this off-season and get to know them a little bit. Then you get to know them a little more. You take an interest in them, not just their baseball careers, but actually get to know them. I like to know what makes these guys tick and how to get the most out of them on the field, and off it.

But it takes time. It doesn't just happen overnight. I mean, why would someone who doesn't know me have an exceptional amount of trust in me? They don't know me, so you build that trust over time, and that's the part I'm looking forward to. And I don't know how it's going to end up, but that's the only way I know how to do it."

In his first season in charge, Baldelli's Twins won 101 of 162 games, a 23-win improvement on the season before. It was the second-most victories in a season in the 119-season history of the franchise. They won 55 games away from home, more than any other team in Major League Baseball, and accumulated a record 308 home runs. For his efforts, Baldelli was named the American League Coach of the Year.

So much for taking time to get to know his players!

Get to know them (Part II)

In five seasons under head coach Dave Roberts, the Los Angeles Dodgers have made the playoffs every year—winning one World Series and losing in the World Series on two other occasions. He is a coach at the top of his game.

When quizzed on how he divides his time with the players given baseball's daily game schedule, Roberts gave a response that will surprise many:

> *"I try to make a point every single day to touch base with every single player. For the most part, though, it's the bench players, role players, or the relief pitchers. The starting pitchers and everyday players are turnkey. It's the guys that are in the bullpen that want to make sure that you love on them and they know their role. Those guys that don't play every day, you want to tell them that you still value them. I want to make sure those guys stay relevant and on board."*

This counterintuitive perspective may not be surprising when you understand Dave Roberts the player. A walk-on in college at UCLA, Roberts went on to have a ten-year career in Major League Baseball, albeit largely as a role player. He won a World Series in 2004 with the Boston Red Sox, becoming a local legend despite not playing in the World Series itself.

A formidable base stealer, Roberts was brought in to pinch-run against the archrival New York Yankees in Game 4 of the American League Championship Series. Despite having not played in over a week, Roberts stole second base and eventually scored, setting in motion an eight-game win streak that would culminate in the Red Sox winning their first championship since 1918.

With this new information, let's revisit Roberts' quote: "Those guys that don't play every day, you want to tell them that you still value them. I want to make sure those guys stay relevant and on board."

The coach who understands the experience of the players at the bottom of the roster is able to foster an environment for everyone, not an environment for the stars. Dave Roberts is creating himself in his team.

Get to know them (Part III)

When Tony Granato took over as head coach of the Colorado Avalanche, he only had three months of experience as an assistant coach. Granato says that the players needed to get back to having fun and they needed a leader they could relate to, which is what made him the ideal choice as their head coach.

So how was he able to haul an underperforming team back into contention? "I spent all my time with players, sitting with Patrick Roy in his hotel room or Joe Sakic in his hotel room and figuring out what they needed to perform," Granato told me.

It's a coaching mindset that Granato still uses even though he's now in charge of his alma mater Wisconsin Badgers. "It goes back to trying to learn what the athlete is like and what they need to get from you. I need them to perform at an elite level for our program to succeed, but they also need something from me. They need to grow and they need to know that I'm looking out for them."

When I pressed Granato on whether today's athlete is different to the previous era, he said yes, and no. "There are certainly more layers to the relationship now, and there's more noise around the players, but it still comes down to building a relationship and gaining their trust," he said. But Granato is quick to acknowledge that every generation is different from the last, and the same humanistic coaching principles apply to a collegiate player that applied when he was coaching Patrick Roy.

"Young players nowadays factor in their brand and their image. Whether you think it's right or wrong, that's the way it is, and you have to understand why it's important to them. Once you know that, you can work with them on how they fit into the overall team. You can't take away part of who they are and what they consider to be valuable, you have to understand it and grow with them," Granato added defiantly.

Some of the most effective coaches of our time have been a generation or two removed from the age of their core playing group, but they're still able to connect on a deep human level. While our veneers change over time, underneath we remain the same connection-seeking humans we've always been.

Go and meet them

Sam Allardyce is best known for assembling one of the English Premier League's most surprising teams. In the early 2000s, Bolton Wanderers became every football fan's second team as the traditional strugglers began attracting some of the game's top players.

In an interview with Simon Mundie on *Don't Tell Me The Score*, Allardyce explained how Bolton were able to attract a world-class player like Youri Djorkaeff, who at the time was a key member of France's all-conquering national team.

"Ultimately, what we did was go and actually meet Youri in his home country. Most teams at the time expected players to come to them," recalled Allardyce. "We had his agent set the meeting and three of our staff jumped on a plane and met the player for two or three hours," he added.

Consider this: Bolton Wanderers created a competitive advantage for themselves by simply going to meet a player in-person before signing him. They cared more.

Djorkaeff's arrival marked a turning point for Bolton's fortunes, with the club going from fighting against relegation to fighting for trophies and European places. Soon after, elite international players began flowing through the doors, with Nigerian captain Jay-Jay Okocha, Spanish internationals Ivan Campo and Fernando Hierro, and French talisman Nicolas Anelka all joining the club.

Campo, in particular—who joined directly from Real Madrid—has heaped praise on Allardyce and the role the coach played in his career resurrection. He told *The Athletic*, "Sam gave me a level of personal affection and care, above everything else professionally, that I will never ever forget."

Allardyce had spent years deliberately building out a huge support staff, putting their talents to use by addressing the international players' human needs as much as their footballing requirements. Allardyce says the club's two player liaisons were deployed to "look after housing, schools, insurance, cars, bank accounts, phones, English lessons, everything, so that the players and their families felt comfortable from day one and they could enjoy coming into work rather than worrying about other issues."

These liaison roles have now become commonplace across professional sport, but it shouldn't be lost on us that as recently as 2002, they were being used to give a minnow club a competitive edge over their rivals.

Bolton weren't merely assembling a football team, they were building connection.

No blame culture

Graham Potter is a head coach who rebelled against what he observed during his career playing in the lower leagues of English soccer. Potter is on record as saying he loved playing football but hated the English obsession with mistakes, and the culture of fear. Tasked with creating something 'different' as head coach of Swedish fourth-tier club Östersunds FK (ÖFK), Potter set about enabling an environment that was the polar opposite to what he'd experienced through his own career. What he built has become known as the 'No Blame Culture'.

To help kickstart the No Blame Culture, ÖFK created a Culture Academy at the club. Each year, players were contractually obligated to put on an artistic performance for the local community. One year it was a rendition of Swan Lake in front of 500 paying guests; another year was a musical act that recognized a local indigenous tribe. These may seem like gimmicks, having grown men navigate an artistic performance is a good way to begin to undo an obsession with mistakes and a culture of fear.

The town of Östersund is a regional outpost in northern Sweden, so the club was unable to attract the same types of players as their rivals from cities like Stockholm and Gothenburg. To compensate, ÖFK built a patchwork roster of second-chancers from England and Sweden, mixed with players from Iran, Iraq, Palestine, Nigeria, Gambia, and Ghana.

In 2018, I spoke to Potter over the phone to ask him how he was able to bring together players from countries with tense political relationships and have them operate harmoniously. "What you find out is that, regardless of where someone is from, at their core, people all want the same things: to be happy, not live in fear, and to be able to provide for their family," he told me.

Potter sees his No Blame Culture as a universal language that allows anyone to thrive. "It's about how you deal with the mistake, and creating an environment that allows you to learn from it," he added.

In his eight seasons coaching Östersunds, Graham Potter led them from the fourth-tier into the first-tier, won the club's first major trophy (the Swedish Cup), and then famously beat Arsenal in a European game in London. (For reference: Arsenal's stadium could seat the entire population of the town of Östersund and have 10,000 seats leftover).

Start with trust

In the first address to his new team, Indianapolis Colts head coach Frank Reich bristled, "One good season is not good enough, I'm just going to tell you that right now." As the 2018 squad looked on attentively, Reich outlined the key ingredients that he saw as necessary for the team to return to being perennial NFL contenders:

1. Trust
2. Toughness
3. Teamwork

Describing his idea of teamwork, Reich said, "It's about us. It's got to be about us." Further defining toughness, he noted, "There's no room for complacency, no room for coasting. Toughness is the relentless drive to get better every day." But it was the conviction behind his first ingredient, trust, that I found enchanting.

Anyone that has led teams knows that trust is a mandatory element of success, but it was especially poignant in this case, given Reich only got the Colts job because their original hire, Josh McDaniels, backed out at the 11th hour.

"Trust is the foundation of everything, and we can't get to where we want to go unless you trust each other, and trust the process," Reich told his players. A mesmerizing orator, Reich had his new charges captivated. He continued, "There is an element of earning each other's trust, but because of the Colts' DNA it means that trust is given. We're going to start with trust."

We're going to start with trust.

And why wouldn't the Colts start with trust? Players that make it to the NFL are put through a stringent vetting process that resembles a covert CIA agent who has the nuclear launch codes.

Under normal circumstances, when any new leader comes into any environment they tend to monitor every single detail until they're fully up to speed. To that type of boss, trust is earned. But if your organization attacks its recruitment process with purpose and is thorough in its cultural development, what reason would there be to be skeptical of your people?

Your people are adults, treat them that way. Start with trust.

Discipline can be a connection tool

In his book *The Culture Code*, author Daniel Coyle explained how former Chicago Cubs head coach Joe Maddon had found a unique way to discipline his players.

"In his office, Maddon keeps a glass bowl filled with slips of paper, each inscribed with the name of an expensive wine," Coyle wrote. "When a player violates a team rule, Maddon asks them to draw a slip of paper out of the bowl, purchase that wine, and uncork it with the coach. In other words, Maddon links the act of discipline to the act of reconnection."

When you sit back and think about it, there are opportunities everywhere for coaches to promote connection, and reconnection. How many can you find in your program?

The connection club

It's well-documented that the San Antonio Spurs have an obsession with partaking of dinner together. The reason is simple: meals—specifically, the ambiance of dinner—create connection. At a dinner restaurant, you sit opposite each other, engage in conversations, and laugh together.

"Dinners help us have a better understanding of each individual person, which brings us closer to each other, and, on the court, understand each other better," former Spurs guard Danny Green said about the famous dinners, which are the brainchild of head coach Gregg Popovich.

On the road, whenever possible, the Spurs stay over and fly out the next morning so they can have that extra time together. Former Spurs center Pau Gasol, who has played for five NBA teams, explained how rare of a cultural artifact it is: "I haven't been a part of something like that anywhere else. The players know how important it is to Pop."

Dinner isn't a high-connection activity only available to Gregg Popovich, or coaches who've won NBA championships. When you take the time to connect with your players and show a little bit of yourself to them (rather than being adversaries), they reciprocate by going out of their way to do things because they know they're important to you.

Belonging

Ultimately, everything in this chapter has been about fostering a sense of belonging in your organization. Fundamentally, human beings want a place that doesn't just welcome them, but quite literally says to them, 'you belong here!'

Gilbert Enoka is the manager of leadership for the All Blacks, and it's belonging (not sweeping the sheds) that he says is the defining feature of their culture. In an interview with longtime All Blacks sponsor Adidas, Enoka addressed the topic:

> *"As the custodian of the All Blacks culture, I make sure everyone has a sense of belonging. When you walk to the pitch, you should feel you belong to this place and that it's fed*

and nourished by the people. Too many organizations focus on the vision and values when they should feed a sense of belonging instead."

A lot of teams do a good job in making players and staff feel welcome when they first arrive, but then it stops. Or worse, it becomes 'you're welcome here when you're performing well'. That's not belonging. That's holding someone ransom.

The 3E's

If there's a holy trinity in modern coaching it's Empathy, Emotion, and Experience.

Throughout this book, we've heard a number of anecdotes from head coaches who've used the holy trinity to guide their teams to enduring success. What's striking about head coaches like Steve Kerr, Pete Carroll, Jürgen Klopp, and Dave Roberts, or environments like the All Blacks, San Antonio Spurs, and Bolton Wanderers, is that they've deliberately infused the 3E's into their programs.

Empathy: How do we show *compassion* for each player's circumstances?

Emotion: How can we infuse *joy* in our practice sessions?

Experience: Our players need to *feel* it, not with the head, but with the *heart*.

The reason coaches would rather obsess over tactics is because people are hard work. Dealing with the messiness of people takes time, it takes energy, and it takes belief. The Xs and Os are easier because lines on a whiteboard never talk back, or feel depressed, or hate their job. But on the other side of this hard work is human connection, and that's where the gold is.

By getting to know your team, getting to know your staff, connecting with them as people, and connecting them to each other, you'll have the right footing to help navigate the ups and downs that are inevitable in elite sport. Rather than on your own, you'll do it together, and you'll create lasting memories whether your team wins or loses.

It's not the tactics. It's the people.

One last reminder

What ends up crippling head coaches is fear. After all that hard work to get to the top job, it's easier to fall in line, do what's been done before, and not stand out. There are societal pressures within the game to 'earn it' by accepting the status quo before you're allowed to shake up the system, show your real personality, or begin to innovate. This legacy thinking handcuffs us and stymies progress.

Vulnerability expert Brené Brown suggests we need more daring leaders, and it's indeed true that we also need more daring coaches. Being a head coach isn't the time to become a shrinking violet, choke up, or conform. Rather, it's a license to be brave, trust your instincts, and show the way. This is why *The Tough Stuff* is written the way it is, because I know you can handle it.

Key Takeaways

1. You don't win because of tactical superiority, you win because your players can executive *whichever tactics you choose* at a faster pace, with consistency and greater intensity, for longer.

2. The organizations that I've seen succeed are those who care more about their people.

3. Even for under-resourced teams, human connection has proven to be a source of competitive advantage in recruiting and on-field success.

4. The holy trinity of coaching is: Empathy, Emotions, Experience.

5. Fear is what cripples most head coaches. Step up and be brave.

"A question all leaders must ask themselves: How am I complicit in creating the conditions I say I don't want?"

Jerry Colonna

The Seven Hard Truths revisited

Now that we've explored the crucial areas to help you navigate *The Tough Stuff*, let's circle back to the hard truths with new eyes and new information.

1. Everyone thinks you're an idiot

Outside pressure is part of elite sport, but you can prepare for the critics and critiques by seeking out opportunities to share your ideas and explain your methods. Rather than building bunkers, build bridges.

2. Your fiercest rival is yourself

Set yourself up to navigate the emotional toll by having a robust support infrastructure around you. The Weight isn't always visible to others, so it's our responsibility to talk about it if we want help carrying the burden.

3. You don't possess the God Particle

You must master the art of letting go of (at least some) control if you are to have longevity as a head coach. Hire great people around you and set them up to be extraordinary.

4. You're not a coach

Figuring out who you are as a person is one of the scariest yet most rewarding journeys for any human. Coaches create themselves in their team, so time spent learning about yourself is time spent researching the future state of your team.

5. You're hired for your brain

The science of decision-making suggests coaches make just about every error in the book. It's time for change. Become a high-performance knowledge worker by rethinking how you spend your time, and what you spend your time on.

6. Every word counts

Including self-talk and behavior in your communication strategy means you'll have a more holistic approach to coaching delivery. Your greatest leap in performance may come from upgrading the vocabulary of your inner voice.

7. Tactics don't really matter

Put the tactical books down, and repurpose that time on designing high-connection, high-cohesion activities for your team. Your tactical execution will improve when your team *know* that you care about them.

About the Author

Cody Royle is the head coach of Canada's national men's AFL team, and the director of coaching for AFL Canada. He has spent the last decade researching, interviewing, and writing about leadership, culture, and performance; and has co-created popular sports websites like InnerVoice, and Bradman Magazine.

This is Cody's second book. His first release, *Where Others Won't*, became highly influential in leadership and elite performance circles. The success of his debut book led to the creation of a podcast of the same name where Cody brings together sports coaches, business executives, and academics, to highlight the real secrets behind the world's best teams.

Guests have included the likes of Joe Dumars, Adam Grant, Patti McCord, Michael Gervais, Chip Wilson, Tasha Eurich, Michael Bungay Stanier, Claude Silver, James Kerr, Rasmus Ankersen, Meg Popovic, Richard Gerver, Howard Behar, Marcus Buckingham, Julian de Guzman, Laura Gassner Otting, and Whitney Johnson. The show was nominated for a Podcast Award in 2019.

You can see more of Cody's work and get in touch with him at his personal website (codyroyle-dot-com). He is also very active on Twitter and LinkedIn.

A native of Melbourne, Australia, Cody lives in Toronto, Canada, with his wife, Stephanie.

Acknowledgements

This book wouldn't have been possible without the help of my accountability partner, Andy Longley, who not only kept me on track but sent me endless neuroscience studies. We're living proof that Aussies and Kiwis can work together.

To Linda Nazareth, Simon Boyce, Russell Earnshaw, and Darragh Boyle, who read an early version of the manuscript and provided me with valuable feedback, your contributions are subtly woven into the final version. Giuseppe Morcinelli and Fredrick Haugen, my cover designer and editor respectively, took my original vision and multiplied it into something even more magical. I thank you both.

I'm fortunate to have three lifelong friends who I get to hear from every day, even from a world away. Nick, Chris, Jim, you've provided me with cheek-hurting laughter and elite mateship for over two decades. I appreciate you guys.

Similarly, I have a band of Aussie brothers here in North America that have supported me through not only the journey of this book, but the ups and downs of life. To Shutts, Cogs, Nabs, Trav, and Dragon, I'll always have your backs, just like you've always had mine.

An unanticipated benefit of writing *Where Others Won't* was that it opened the door to new bonds that I wouldn't have made otherwise. In particular, I've received daily support and friendship from great men like Joe Dumars, Fergus Connolly, Brian Levenson, Marty Lauzon, Aidan McCullen, and Darren Burgess.

I have three great women in my life, all of whom I can turn to when I need a hug, or a reminder to back myself. To Stephanie, Deborah, and Teresa, I'm lucky to have a number one cheerleader whether I'm in North America, Australia, or Europe. I love you all.

Last of all, I want to thank my team, the Bloods. A lot of the themes of this book were inspired by how you guys carry yourselves. I've achieved some wonderful things in footy, and in life, but there's a reason "Head Coach of AFL Team Canada" is how I describe myself when people ask. Being your coach is the most rewarding thing I get to do.

References

Books

Where Others Won't: Taking People Innovation from the Locker Room into the Boardroom by Cody Royle (Independent, 2017)

Thinking In Bets: Making Smarter Decisions When You Don't Have All The Facts by Annie Duke (Portfolio, 2019)

My Life and Rugby: The Autobiography by Eddie Jones (Macmillan, 2019)

The Happiness Track: How to Apply the Science of Happiness to Accelerate Your Success by Emma Seppälä (HarperOne, 2016)

Fooled by Randomness: The Hidden Role of Chance in Life and in the Markets by Nassim Nicholas Taleb (Random House, 2001)

Shift Your Mind: 9 Mental Shifts to Thrive in Preparation and Performance by Brian Levenson (Disruption Books, 2020)

Living on the Volcano: The Secrets of Surviving as a Football Manager by Michael Calvin (Cornerstone Digital, 2015)

The Landmarks of Tomorrow by Peter Drucker (Transaction Publishers; First Edition, 1996)

Wisdom at Work: The Making of a Modern Elder by Chip Conley (Currency, 2018)

"Entrepreneurial Leadership: The Art of Launching New Ventures, Inspiring Others, and Running Stuff" by Joel C. Peterson (HarperCollins, 2020)

"The Process: The Methodology, Philosophy & Principles of Coaching Winning Teams" by Fergus Connolly and Cam Josse (Independent, 2019)

Practical Modern Basketball by John Wooden (Pearson; Third Edition, 1998)

The Making of a Leader: What Elite Sport Can Teach Us About Leadership, Management and Performance by Tom Young (Robinson, 2020)

Start with Why: How Great Leaders Inspire Everyone to Take Action by Simon Sinek (Portfolio, 2009)

The Score Takes Care of Itself: My Philosophy of Leadership by Bill Walsh, Craig Walsh, and Steve Jamison (Portfolio, 2009)

Multipliers: How the Best Leaders Make Everyone Smarter by Liz Wiseman (Harper, 2017)

The Culture Code: The Secrets of Highly Successful Groups by Daniel Coyle (Bantam, 2018)

Podcasts

Where Others Won't: Season 1, Episode 3 with Paul Roos and James Kerr

Where Others Won't: Season 1, Episode 18 with Michael Lombardi

Where Others Won't: Season 2, Episode 1 with Tasha Eurich

Where Others Won't: Season 2, Episode 8 with Stuart Lancaster

Where Others Won't: Season 2, Episode 11 with Roy Rana

Where Others Won't: Season 2, Episode 33 with Kirk Ferentz

Where Others Won't: Season 2, Episode 34 with Tony Granato

Where Others Won't: Season 3, Episode 2 with Lisa Alexander

Where Others Won't: Season 3, Episode 5 with Scott Robertson

The High Performance Podcast: Season 1, Episode 3 with Mauricio Pochettino

The High Performance Podcast: Season 2, Episode 1 with Ole Gunnar Solskjaer

The High Performance Podcast: Season 3, Episode 1 with Steven Gerrard

The Tim Ferriss Show: Episode 444 with Hugh Jackman

Modern Soccer Coach: Jesse Marsch – Inside His Red Bull Environment

Flying Coach: Two Champions on Mentors, Philosophies, and Why They Coach

Flying Coach: Buying into Analytics and The Advantage of the Multisport Athlete with Dave Roberts

Don't Tell Me The Score: Managing People with Sam Allardyce

Brukie and Burgo - The Podcast: Justin Langer

Brukie and Burgo - The Podcast: The Burgo Story, Part 3

Articles

"Q&A: John Fox takes us inside the spinning world of an NFL head coach, from the first interview to the hot seat" by Jay Glazer (*The Athletic*, Jan 4, 2019)

"Frank Lampard on being a manager: You have to practise, fail, get better" (BBC.com, Nov 18, 2020)

"Most valuable traits of an NFL head coach? Eight star players weigh in" by Jim Trotter (NFL.com, Jul 7, 2020)

"The man who made sure Ange Postecoglou wasn't lost in translation" by Vince Rugari (*Brisbane Times*, Dec 6, 2019)

"Pochettino worried by impact of Amazon documentary at Tottenham" (Fotmob.com, Undated)

"England boss Gareth Southgate: 'Draconian/ rules not suitable for players" by Phil McNulty (BBC.com, Dec 1, 2016)

"Why The Yankees Are Crowdsourcing Their Manager Vetting Process" by Billy Witz (*New York Times*, Nov 20, 2017)

"90 minutes with Pep Guardiola - Part 3" translated into English by Alex Clapham for Caño Football (interview on GOL, undated)

"Guardiola's hypocrisy over Man City's owner undermines his pleas about Catalonia" (*New Statesman*, Mar 13, 2018)

"Why Lynx coach Cheryl Reeve has vowed to assemble an all-female coaching staff for 2020 — and beyond" by Pat Borzi (MinnPost, Jan 17, 2020)

"AFL coaches need to focus on their mental health, says ex-Carlton coach Brendon Bolton" by Alister Nicholson and Luke Pentony (ABC, Dec 7, 2019)

"NBA playoffs: The Miami Heat's Duncan Robinson steps into the sunlight" by Ramona Shelburne (ESPN.com, Sep 2, 2020)

"Marcelo Bielsa admits Leeds have spied on every opponent this season" by Louise Taylor (*The Guardian*, Jan 16, 2019)

"A week in the life of a coach" by Kevin Van Valkenburg (ESPN, Nov 22, 2013)

"NBA's scary secret: Job stress is destroying the health of some of the best coaches" by Dan Woike (*Los Angeles Times*, Dec 7, 2019)

"Michael Malone: Shame on NBA for not allowing coaches' families in bubble" by Royce Young (ESPN.com, Sep 4, 2020)

"Montgomery thankful for 'deserved' firing" (TSN.ca, May 25, 2020)

"How Scott Van Pelt and CC Sabathia helped Steve Sarkisian decide to get sober" by Will Brinson (CBS Sports, Jun 8, 2017)

"Buckley's self-discovery takes him within sight of the holy grail" by Jake Niall (*The Age*, Sep 28, 2018)

"The 'problematic' word that 'triggered' Nathan Buckley's blast" (7 Sport, Aug 31, 2020)

"Phoenix Mercury's globe-trotting coach is mom first" by Kara G. Morrison (*Raising Arizona Kids*, Jul 1, 2016)

"I Failed Tremendously: Hue Jackson on the Blues After the Browns" by Greg Bishop (Sports Illustrated, Aug 22, 2019)

"Jürgen Klopp: on clothes, the keys to coaching and Liverpool team talks" by Jacob Steinberg (*The Guardian*, May 21, 2020)

"Liverpool's Pep Lijnders: 'Our identity is intensity. It comes back in every drill'" by Arthur Renard (*The Guardian*, Dec 2, 2019)

"Your Brain Is Not for Thinking" by Lisa Feldman Barrett (*New York Times*, Nov 23, 2020)

"The Army Rolls Out a New Weapon: Strategic Napping" by Dave Philipps (*New York Times*, Oct 1, 2020)

"The Busier You Are, the More You Need Quiet Time" by Justin Talbot-Zorn and Leigh Marz (Mar 17, 2017)

"Airbnb's Chip Conley is doubling down on being a modern elder" by Melissa Locker (*Fast Company*, Oct 23, 2018)

"RB Salzburg's Jesse Marsch: When I see videos of myself trying to speak German it's embarrassing" by Lawrence Ostlere (*The Independent*, Dec 10, 2019)

"All Blacks: Steve Hansen's secret - what the All Blacks don't do on game day" by Liam Napier (NZ Herald, Nov 10, 2018)

"Sorry folks ... Delaware is closed" by (Delaware Online, Jan 16, 2014)

"The ex-Wallabies prop unpicking the secrets of rugby" by Rhiannon Garth Jones (RugbyPass, Jun 23, 2020)

"Twins' Rocco Baldelli, 38, named AL Manager of the Year" by Bradford Doolittle (ESPN, Nov 12, 2019)

"'Big Sam was miles ahead of his time' – when Bolton's Galacticos upset the elite" by Oliver Kay, Adam Crafton and Jack Lang (*The Athletic*, Mar 28, 2020)

"San Diego Loyal manager 'proud' of walk-off over alleged homophobic abuse" (*The Guardian*, Oct 1, 2020)

"How Ostersund's 'no blame' culture took club from fourth division to Europa League" by James Olley (*Evening Standard*, Feb 15, 2018)

"Meet Graham Potter - the Englishman using Swan Lake and rock concerts to lead a tiny Swedish club to glory over Galatasaray" (*The Telegraph*, Jul 19, 2017)

"Michelin restaurants and fabulous wines: Inside the secret team dinners that have built the Spurs' dynasty" by Baxter Holmes (ESPN, Apr 18, 2019)

"Make mental strength your strongest skill - The All Blacks Way" by Maria Nokkonen (Gameplan A, Mar 1, 2017)

Videos, Shows, Films, Songs, and Academic Papers

"Bill Belichick on Trump Friendship" by ABC News via YouTube

"Saban on second chances" by AL.com via YouTube

"Emotional Parker proud of Fulham season" by Sky Sports

The Playbook: "Doc Rivers" by Netflix

The Playbook: "Jill Ellis" by Netflix

"Guardiola reveals the worst part of his job as Man City manager" by SoccerAM via YouTube

"Lonely" by Justin Bieber and Benny Blanco (*Friends Keep Secrets*, Def Jam Recordings and Interscope Records, 2020)

"Steve Kerr on having Warriors players coach during timeouts" by ESPN via YouTube

"The Newest Zealander Visits PM Jacinda Ardern" by *The Late Show with Steven Colbert* via YouTube

"All or Nothing: Manchester City" by Amazon Prime Video

"Lera Boroditsky: How language shapes the way we think" by TED Talks

Any Given Sunday by Oliver Stone (Warner Bros., 1999)

"Doc Rivers: Rah-rah speeches are very overrated" by ESPN

The Test by Amazon Prime Video

"Cultural variation in eye movements during scene perception" by Hannah Faye Chua, Julie E. Boland, and Richard E. Nisbett (Department of Psychology, University of Michigan, 2005)

"Coach Frank Reich's First Team Meeting" by NFL via Facebook Watch

Personal Interviews

Dan Quinn
Darren Burgess
Andy Friend
Ben Olsen
Tom Morris
Jay Triano
Carly Clarke
Dr. Meeta Singh
Dr. Amy Kruse
Pratik Patel
Jamion Christian
Graham Potter